NEW MERMAIDS

General editors:
William C. Carroll, Boston University
Brian Gibbons, University of Münster
Tiffany Stern, University of Oxford

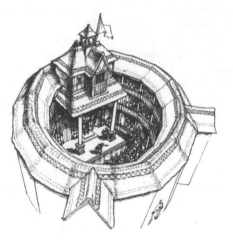

Reconstruction of an Elizabethan theatre
by C. Walter Hodges

NEW MERMAIDS

NEW MERMAIDS

ELIZABETH CARY

THE TRAGEDY OF MARIAM

THE FAIR QUEEN OF JEWRY

Edited by Karen Britland

University of Wisconsin–Madison

methuen | drama

LONDON · NEW YORK · OXFORD · NEW DELHI · SYDNEY

METHUEN DRAMA
Bloomsbury Publishing Plc
50 Bedford Square, London, WC1B 3DP, UK
1385 Broadway, New York, NY 10018, USA
29 Earlsfort Terrace, Dublin 2, Ireland

BLOOMSBURY, METHUEN DRAMA and the Methuen Drama logo are
trademarks of Bloomsbury Publishing Plc

A catalogue record for this book is available from the British Library.

A catalog record for this book is available from the Library of Congress.

ISBN: PB: 978-0-7136-8876-4
ePDF: 978-1-4081-4378-0
eBook: 978-1-4081-4379-7

Series: New Mermaids

Printed and bound in Great Britain

To find out more about our authors and books visit www.bloomsbury.com
and sign up for our newsletters.

CONTENTS

ACKNOWLEDGEMENTS

Working on this edition has been great fun, not least because of the people who have helped it along the way. I first read *The Tragedy of Mariam* in 1995 in Diane Purkiss's MA class, and I am grateful to her for sparking an interest in early modern women's drama that has given me a career. I have since taught the play to both graduates and undergraduates and I am truly grateful to everyone who studied in my classes for their enthusiasm and their challenging ideas. Nancy Simpson-Younger, Kristiane Stapleton and Marshelle Woodward deserve particular mention: I have benefited immensely from their thoughts about early modern women's writing.

My colleagues at Keele University and the University of Wisconsin–Madison generously allowed me time to work on this edition, and I would not have been up to the task if it had not been for the experience I gained working for Martin Butler on the Cambridge edition of the *Complete Works of Ben Jonson*. As ever, Martin: thank you. Bill Carroll has been a wonderful general editor, as well as a co-enthusiast for beer and *Mad Men*. I thank him for his fine advice, encouragement and hospitality. Anna Brewer at A&C Black has been amazingly tolerant and fun to work with, and Sue Gibbons's sharp eye has spotted more than its share of mistakes. I am immensely lucky to have encountered both of them.

Finally, only my family and close friends know what a nightmare I am when confronted with a deadline. My parents can't get rid of me, but a million thanks must go to David Como for putting up with it, and for being a far better laugh than King Herod.

Karen Britland

In memory of my grandmothers
Edith Jenkins, 1909–1996
and
Miriam Britland, 1902–1996

INTRODUCTION

About the Play

The Tragedy of Mariam by Elizabeth Cary, Lady Falkland, was the first original play by a woman published in English and marks an important place in the history of women's writing. It tells the story of King Herod and his wife, Mariam, and places an unusual emphasis on female speech, linking it in various ways to ideas of tyranny, judgement, marriage and divorce. In her opening soliloquy, for example, Mariam considers the notion of deceit and, drawing attention to cultural assumptions about women's inconstancy, places the blame firmly with women's husbands. By beginning her play with a woman's soliloquy and engaging with debates about female speech, Cary clearly signals her desire to explore the constraints of early modern gender ideologies. The play therefore provides valuable first-hand evidence of an early modern woman's negotiation of the cultural mores that urged upon her chastity, silence and obedience.

Mariam's interest in marital jealousy, race, deceit and female silence has led to comparisons with Shakespeare's *Othello*.[1] Cary's play was not, however, written for the commercial theatre, and may not have been intended for performance at all. Early critical work has emphasised its status as a play designed for reading, relying heavily on a biography of Cary, written by one of her daughters, to posit that it reflected its author's experience of early modern marriage. More recent critics have challenged the idea that the play is not performable, while others have emphasised the multiple perspectives *Mariam* gives on marriage, arguing that Cary's education led her to absorb certain attitudes about female chastity and submission.

Mariam is an extremely complicated play that, like Shakespearean drama, never provides a single perspective on any issue. It is important to literary studies because it was written by a woman and, for this reason, an extended biographical section about Cary is provided here. However, the play is also fascinating in its own right: it evinces a forceful understanding of literary genre and rhetorical form; it adheres to the classical unities of time and place; and it provides a debate on gender roles that affects our understanding, not only of the early modern family, but of women's political and public place within seventeenth-century society.

---

1 Weller and Ferguson suggest *Mariam* might echo or anticipate *Othello*: p. 41 and p. 174, note 68.

Summary of the Plot

Mariam begins the play alone, lamenting. She recants her former accusations towards Julius Caesar who wept at the death of Pompey, noting she now knows one can be both happy and sad about the death of a respected enemy. She explains she has often wished for the death of Herod, who murdered her brother and grandfather and who, she has discovered, ordered her own execution if he died. She admits his jealousy has cost him her love, but asserts she has always been chaste. Her lament ends with an admission that she owes Herod her grief because of his deep love for her, but she suppresses her tears because Alexandra, her mother, is approaching. In I.ii, Alexandra reproaches Mariam for weeping and curses Herod for the murders of her son and father, noting that Herod is so fickle he might cast off Mariam and return to Doris, his former wife. Mariam refutes this possibility, explaining that Herod has bypassed his first-born son and promised the throne to her son, Alexander. Her mother is appalled because she believes Alexander, through his genealogy, is already heir to the throne.

Salome, Herod's sister, enters (I.iii) and accuses Mariam and Alexandra of plotting. The three women argue about social precedence and Mariam accuses Salome of arranging the death of her first husband so she could marry Constabarus. Salome is left alone (I.iv) and privately admits she is in love with the Arabian, Silleus, and wishes to be rid of Constabarus. She laments that women are forbidden to apply for divorce and wishes Herod were alive so she could denounce Constabarus for protecting the condemned sons of Baba. Silleus arrives (I.v) and Salome explains that, against all custom, she will seek a divorce from Constabarus. Constabarus then appears (I.vi) and chides Salome for talking with Silleus. Salome rounds on him, denigrates his low birth and declares she is going to obtain a divorce. The Chorus conclude the first act by declaring that vacillating minds will never find contentment.

In II.i, Pheroras looks forward to his long-awaited marriage with Graphina. He exhorts Graphina to speak, noting that 'silence is a sign of discontent' and seeking her acquiescence to their marriage. Graphina replies that she requites Pheroras's affection. Constabarus arrives with the sons of Baba whom he has been protecting (II.ii). The eldest son questions the rumours of Herod's death and Constabarus accuses him of cowardice, but the younger son admits it is likely Caesar will pardon Herod. Doris, Herod's former wife, follows next with her son, bemoaning her exile and praying for revenge against Mariam (II.iii). Her son suggests they should murder Mariam's children, but Doris prefers to remain apart and lament. Next, Silleus tries to provoke Constabarus into a fight over

Salome (II.iv). Constabarus will not engage for such a low cause, but fights and wounds Silleus once the latter has called him a coward. The Chorus debate the question of judgement, noting that, because everyone wants Herod dead, everyone believes him to be so.

In Act III, Salome chides Pheroras for his marriage to Graphina until Ananell, the priest, approaches. Ananell declares Herod is not dead (III.ii), and Salome blackmails Pheroras into denouncing Constabarus to Herod. Mariam receives the news of Herod's return (III.iii) and announces she will no longer share a bed with him. The Chorus insist that a wife's body and thoughts are her husband's. Herod then arrives with his attendants, looking forward to seeing Mariam (IV.i). He is greeted by Pheroras who accuses Constabarus of harbouring Baba's sons (IV.ii). Herod condemns Constabarus and the sons to death, while Pheroras informs him Salome has divorced her husband. In IV.iii, Mariam finally arrives, but does not reciprocate Herod's welcome. He chides her for her perversity, but she explains she cannot act differently from the way she feels. They are interrupted by a butler, carrying a love potion he claims is for Herod from Mariam (IV.iv). Herod suspects the drink is poisoned, accuses Mariam of being unchaste and has her carried away to execution. The butler, alone, admits he has been working for Salome and laments his part in Mariam's downfall (IV.v).

In IV.vi, Constabarus and Baba's sons rail against women as they are taken off to die. Herod vacillates over how Mariam should be killed, until Salome exits to command the execution herself (IV.vii). Mariam laments her mistakes, realising Herod would still love her if she had not been improvident. She is met by Doris who curses her and accuses her of living with Herod in adultery (IV.viii). The Chorus to Act IV preach forgiveness and humility in the face of adversity.

In Act V, Herod receives the news of Mariam's death and is informed that the butler has hanged himself. He realises Mariam was innocent and dreams of bringing her back to life. The Chorus remind us of the play's adherence to the unity of time and suggest its events should be taken as a warning to posterity.

Date and Sources

Date

The Tragedy of Mariam was entered in the Stationers' Register on 17 December 1612 and published by Richard Hawkins in 1613. It is thought to have been written sometime after 1602 because its main source (see below) was published that year. Two copies of the printed text carry a dedication 'To Diana's Earthly Deputess, and my worthy sister, Mistress Elizabeth Cary', stating that the dedicatee is a 'moon' to the author, while her 'fair brother' is a sun. This dedication has been the prime engine for dating the play, although the results are inconclusive. Henry Cary, Elizabeth Cary's husband, had two female relatives called Elizabeth: his sister, married to Sir John Saville in 1586 and afterwards known as Lady Saville; and his sister-in-law, Elizabeth (née Bland), wife of his brother Philip. It is usually assumed that *Mariam*'s dedicatee is Elizabeth Bland Cary, and that the text was written before 1605 when Philip was knighted, thereafter making his wife Lady Cary. However, no date has been established for the marriage of Philip and Elizabeth, whose first child was not baptised until 1610. Indeed, G. E. Cokayne, in his work on the Bland family, can only place the marriage 'in or shortly before 1609'.[2] It is possible that the couple did not marry until Philip had received his knighthood, which would mean that Elizabeth Bland was never, technically, Mistress Cary. However, Elizabeth Cary, the author, undoubtedly spent time with her Bland Cary in-laws for they all lived in Hertfordshire with the Cary family until 1612 when the Bland Carys moved to St Olave's in London.[3]

Meredith Skura has suggested Cary probably wrote *Mariam* before the birth of her first child in 1609, while Barbara Lewalski notes that references in the dedication to Phoebus's sojourn in the Antipodes seem to refer to Henry Cary's 'military adventures and imprisonment' (1604–6).[4] It is also notable that Henry Cary danced as a Knight of Apollo in Campion's *Lord Hay's Masque* in January 1607, a fact that might contribute to the dedication's references to Apollo and Phoebus. If this is plausible, it would date the dedication to no earlier than the winter of 1606–7, and the play's composition to no later than 1609.

Sources

Mariam is strongly influenced by *A History in Twenty Books, wherein the Antiquity of the Jews is Discovered*, included in Thomas Lodge's translation of the *Famous and Memorable Works of Josephus* (1602). Cary made use predominantly of Book 15 of the *Antiquity of the Jews* which contains the murder of Mariam's brother and the queen's own demise. There are

2 G. E. Cokayne, 'Bland, of Carleton, co. York', *The Genealogist* n.s. 23 (1907), p. 201.
3 Cokayne cites baptism records for two children in Aldenham and Great Berkhampstead, Herts, in 1610 and 1611 respectively. Subsequent baptisms took place at St Olave's: Cokayne, op.cit., p. 202.
4 Meredith Skura, 'The reproduction of mothering in *Mariam, Queen of Jewry*: a defense of "biographical" criticism', *Tulsa Studies in Women's Literature* 16.1 (1997), p. 48; Barbara Lewalski, *Writing Women in Jacobean England*, 1993, p. 190.

numerous points in her text where the influence of Lodge is very clear. For example, the play's opening Argument tells us that Mariam 'bare the death of her friends exceeding hardly', a paraphrase of the *Antiquity*'s, 'She digested also the loss of her friends very hardly'.[5]

Also striking are the play's allusions to biblical stories, particularly from the Old Testament and Apocrypha. In Act I, which establishes the importance of Mariam's genealogy, allusion is made to material from the books of Genesis, Exodus, 1 Kings, 2 Esdras, and Deuteronomy. It seems Cary deliberately limited her references to New Testament verses to ensure the relative authenticity of her historical story. This also means that when post-Christian allusions are made, particularly in Act V around Mariam's execution and the butler's suicide, they are all the more striking.

Mariam was influenced by the genre of closet drama (see below) and critics have perceived in it allusions to the Countess of Pembroke's translation of Robert Garnier's *Marc-Antoine* (1592) and, perhaps, Samuel Daniel's *Cleopatra* (1594). The play also bears the marks of Cary's humanist education: Mariam's vacillation between grief and joy at Herod's death was probably inspired by Montaigne, while Constabarus's speech on friendship might draw on Erasmus (see I.i.10n. and II.ii.14–22n.). Finally, it is possible that Cary consulted the Mariam story either in Christine de Pisan's *City of Ladies* or its Latin inspiration, Boccaccio's *De mulieribus claris*.

The Play

Genre and structure

The Tragedy of Mariam is usually described as 'closet drama', a term coined in the nineteenth century to describe plays not written for the commercial stage. Jonas Barish has usefully listed the characteristics of such works, noting they share an interest in simple plots from historical sources, favour long speeches and soliloquies, and contain characters such as messengers who provide an insight into off-stage action.[6] They usually observe a five-act structure and, like *Mariam*, begin a new scene when a new character enters or leaves. Each of the five acts is followed by a chorus that comments on the action, and the play unrolls in a single geographical location and within a set time span (usually a day). *Mariam*, for example, emphasises its adherence to the unity of time: the chorus to Act V comments on the play's time span and a lovely symmetry is established

---

5 *Antiquity*, 15.11.399.
6 Jonas Barish, 'Language for the study, language for the stage', *The Elizabethan Theatre XII*, ed. A. L. Magnusson and C. E. McGee, 1993, p. 20.

which sees Mariam's opening disquisition on weeping reflected in Herod's lamentation for his wife's death.

England had a long tradition of plays not written for the commercial stage. Students were encouraged to read and perform classical drama as part of their education, and scholars such as John Studley and Jasper Heywood published English translations of Latin plays. This practice did not just apply to boys: in the mid-1500s, Jane, Lady Lumley, who had been tutored at home, translated Euripedes's *Iphigeneia* out of the Greek. It has long been suggested, however, that Elizabeth Cary's *Mariam* should be connected, not with these school exercises, but with the kind of drama advocated by the Countess of Pembroke, sister to the famous Elizabethan poet, Sir Philip Sidney.

In 1592, Pembroke published her *Antonius*, a translation of Robert Garnier's neo-classical French play, *Marc-Antoine*. It contained a prose Argument explaining the play's action, a list of 'The Actors', and concluded four of its five acts with a chorus. Two years later, Samuel Daniel, one of the Countess's clients, published his *Cleopatra*; Samuel Brandon, an admirer of Daniel, then published his *Tragicomedy of the Virtuous Octavia* (1598); and, in 1605, Daniel brought out his *Philotas* (for which he was called to account because it was thought to allude to the downfall of the Earl of Essex). Other plays preceding the publication of *Mariam*, usually classed as closet drama, include Thomas Kyd's *Cornelia* (1594), Sir William Alexander's tragedies, and Fulke Greville's *Mustapha* (1609). These plays all share structural similarities and, as Marta Straznicky has noted, their authors were all associated with the Sidney family.[7] It is usually suggested that Elizabeth Cary was introduced to closet drama by Michael Drayton, who was friends with Daniel.

Over the years, closet drama has become associated with privacy and élitism, and, because its plays are deemed appropriate for reading alone or in small groups in a private house, is considered a genre particularly suitable for women. However, recent work has shown that the manuscript circulation of such texts should not necessarily be seen as more private than print.[8] A vast variety of sermons, poems, letters and other handwritten documents circulated around the country and across Europe, were copied out in part or in whole, were re-circulated, re-copied and passed on again. As Diane Purkiss has noted, 'Senecan "private" drama could be much more dangerously "public" or political than plays for the

---

7 Marta Straznicky, *Privacy, Playreading, and Women's Closet Drama, 1550–1700*, 2004, p. 49.

8 See, for example, Adam Smyth's work on the intersection of print and manuscript texts, *Profit and Delight: Printed Miscellanies in England, 1640–1682*, 2004, especially chapter 3.

public stage, because it did not have to pass the scrutiny of the Revels office'.[9] If there is a difference between this kind of manuscript circulation and that of printed texts, it is perhaps less one that juxtaposes privacy against publicity, but one that contrasts gift-exchange with the commercial market place. In other words, the concerns of closet drama are as much those of class as of gender. Cary certainly uses closet drama to interrogate the propriety of women's speech, but, in doing so, she also evinces a deep understanding of the possibilities of the genre which, as Karen Raber has noted, deconstructs the categories of privacy and publicity, amateur and professional, used to maintain gender boundaries.[10] Her play might not have been destined for performance at the Globe theatre, but that makes it neither intrinsically private, domestic nor apolitical. Indeed, by 1611, the manuscript of *Mariam* may well have found its way out of Cary's family circle and into the hands of the King's Men's acting company.[11] Writing a play for manuscript circulation did not prevent an author from placing herself within, and being acknowledged by, a wider literary culture.

Mariam, for example, evinces a strong awareness of other literary genres, deployed, in the main, to assist characterisation. Doris, Herod's rejected first wife, wishes the play were a revenge tragedy. At her first entrance, she prays for vengeance (II.iii.33) and her son offers to devise a 'subtle, hidden plot' to exterminate Mariam's children (II.iii.59–60). Later, she is perceived as a 'spirit sent to drive [Mariam] to despair' (IV.viii.56), and calls down a curse on the queen, asserting, 'Had I ten thousand tongues and every tongue / Inflamed with poison's power and steeped in gall, / My curses would not answer for my wrong' (IV.viii.85–7). Like Queen Margaret in Shakespeare's *Richard III*, she infects the play with her past, her curses – with their supernatural implications – troubling its linear, historical discourse (see IV.viii.77–9).

Similarly, an awareness of genre is deployed to flesh out the character of Silleus. From his first entrance in I.v, Silleus uses the hyperbolic language of romantic love, prevalent in Elizabethan poetry. Entranced by Salome, he terms her 'beauty's queen', 'rare creature' and 'Asia's miracle' (I.v.23, 31), and, in true romance fashion, believes she loves him only

---

9 Purkiss, p. xviii.
10 Karen Raber, *Dramatic Difference: Gender, Class, and Genre in the Early Modern Closet Drama*, 2001, p. 23.
11 *Mariam* might be a source for the anonymous *Second Maiden's Tragedy*, entered in the Stationers' Register in 1611: see Weller and Ferguson, p. 6. See also Donald W. Foster, 'A Funeral Elegy: W[illiam] S[hakespeare]'s "Best-Speaking Witnesses"', *Publications of the Modern Language Association* 111.5 (1996), pp. 1080–1105.

because he loved her first (I.v.42–3). Later, like a chivalric hero, he tries to defends Salome's reputation from Constabarus, asserting his sword 'owes his service to her sacred name' (II.iv.26). The scene juxtaposes Constabarus's jaded view of Salome against Silleus's idealism, and, like Shakespeare's mockery of Petrarchism at the start of Romeo and Juliet, reveals the naïvety of this overblown romantic discourse. It also establishes parallels between Silleus's love for Salome and Herod's love for Mariam. When he enters in Act IV, Herod calls for his wife in Silleus's language, terming her 'rare creature' and a 'miracle' (IV.i.10, 28). This excessive woman-worship is clearly presented as problematic, leading, as it does, to personal and political instability.

Ilona Bell has noted that Cary's play contains numerous sonnets, arguing that it 'offers a counterpoint to Renaissance literary convention' because it foregrounds Mariam's speech and explores the ways in which the female audience of male-authored poems 'influenced male lyric and dramatic tradition'.[12] Mariam certainly punctures the pretensions of Petrarchan discourse as both Salome and Mariam speak out against, manipulate, or try to evade, the subject positions it offers them. It is perhaps worth remembering that Cary was related, through her mother, to Sir Thomas Wyatt, the famous Tudor sonneteer. While it is plausible that Cary modelled herself, in part, on the Countess of Pembroke when she chose to write a closet drama, we should not forget she had literary forebears of her own. The prevalence of the sonnet form throughout Mariam not only emphasises the play's engagement with certain types of poetic discourse, but signals a family allegiance (Wyatt's poetry seems, for example, to be echoed at II.iv.39). Much like Mary Wroth's engagement with Sidnean romance, the prevalence of sonnets in the play is at once Cary's reworking of a masculinist literary tradition, and an acknowledgement of that tradition's connection to her family.

Marriage and divorce

Mariam is acutely concerned with issues of marriage and divorce, dealing not only with Mariam's marital disputes with Herod, but with the implications of Herod's divorce from Doris and Salome's desires to rid herself of Constabarus. The play provides perspectives on marriage and divorce from all angles: we see Alexandra's situation as a widow and former queen; we hear Doris lament her post-divorce dispossession; we witness Mariam's discontent with her husband; we are party to Herod's desire for his wife and to Constabarus's distress over Salome's infidelities; we see Pheroras's joy at marrying Graphina and witness her careful submission

12 Bell, pp. 19–20.

to her husband. In addition, the play's various choruses, particularly the third, provide a commentary on the characters' actions, colouring our judgement about marriage by such *sententiae* as "Tis not enough for one that is a wife / To keep her spotless from an act of will, / But from suspicion she should free her life / And bare herself of power as well as will' (Chorus III.97–100).

The third chorus promulgates the idea of the *femme couverte*, or 'covered wife', whose legal rights are subsumed beneath those of her husband. Leaning on biblical texts such as Ephesians 5.22–3, which commands wives to 'be obedient to their husbands' and to submit because 'the man [is] head of the woman in marriage', the chorus asserts a wife's thoughts are not her own (Chorus III.119–20). However, taken as a whole, Cary's play interrogates this idea, showing it to be an impossibility. In Karen Raber's words, 'The lines that are drawn dispossess [Mariam] of herself, making her the property of her husband, but only in an unstable and embattled way'.[13] From the first, Mariam is torn by conflicting obligations (to her husband; to her mother; to her murdered relations; to social custom), and the play underlines this, both through its presentation of her inner conflicts and in the way it scatters different modes of behaviour among its female characters. As Andrew Hiscock has observed, 'Cary exploits the dynamic, multivocal nature of dramatic discourse in order to probe in particular the irresolvable inconsistencies in cultural expectations of female experience'.[14]

There is a fundamental paradox in social injunctions towards women's selfless obedience: if one is exhorted to submit one's will entirely to one's husband, the implication is that there is a self and a will that must be given up. Indeed, the act of submission itself implies an act of will. Cary's play persistently dramatises this paradox, drawing attention to the splitting and fragmentation it engenders in its female subjects.[15] When Salome regrets that her tongue 'To Constabarus by itself is tied' (I.iv.17–18), she draws attention to this process, participating in a literary and cultural form that particularises women. The Petrarchan trope of blazon, deployed in Elizabethan love poetry, praised a woman's parts (her lips, her brow, her hair), without providing an overarching sense of a whole person. Here, Salome's tongue, acting apparently on its own, draws Salome into an invidious marriage that leaves her further split from herself and her desires. In other words, the play draws attention to the

---

13 Raber, op.cit., p. 158.
14 Andrew Hiscock, 'The hateful cuckoo', *Forum for Modern Language Studies* 33.2 (1997), p. 99.
15 See Raber, op.cit., pp. 158–9.

conflicts this kind of love discourse engenders for women, at the same time as it allows Salome – who consciously draws on the discourse of Petrarchan fragmentation – partially to absolve herself of responsibility for her marriage.

Sohemus, Mariam's friend and adviser, acknowledges the contradictions inherent in cultural constructions of women and their voices when he worries that unbridled speech will 'endanger [Mariam] without desert' (III.iii.65–6). Acknowledging the convention that sees a woman's public speech as analogous to sexual licence, the play seeks to decouple speech and sex by demonstrating Mariam's sexual purity at the same time as it accords her a voice. At the end of the play, however, Mariam takes responsibility for her transgressions, recognising she should have pursued both chastity and humility, and not just relied on a private knowledge of her own sexual continence (IV.viii.35–45). At the same time, the play's presentation of the irrepressibly loquacious Salome, whose unbridled speech leads her into adultery and brings about the downfall of two husbands, affirms, as Margaret Ferguson notes, 'the ideological link between unruly female bodies and unruly tongues'.[16]

Salome is a character whose opinions we would be advised not to trust. However, the play shows us she *is* trusted, and by none other than Judea's king, the ostensible locus of authority and law. By taking issue with biblical texts such as Deuteronomy 24.1, which makes a 'bill of divorcement' a strictly masculine privilege, as well as with Josephus's *Antiquity*, which insists it 'is only lawful for the husband' to divorce, Salome marks herself as an unruly threat, not only to the structures of patriarchal marriage, but also, obliquely, to Herod's authority.[17] In a consummate circularity, Cary's play calls into question the authority that maintains divorce as a masculine privilege, at the same time as it appears to uphold injunctions against unruly women's disruptive potential.

Jeanne Addison Roberts has noted that marriage and divorce were urgent issues in the years before *Mariam* was composed, and again in 1613 when the play was printed.[18] On 14 November 1605, Sir Robert Rich was granted a divorce from his wife, Penelope (née Devereux), who had been having an affair with Sir Charles Blount for half a decade.[19] Sir Robert was the landlord of much of St Bartholomew-the-Great and his

---

16 Margaret Ferguson, 'A room not their own', *The Comparative Perspective on Literature*, ed. Clayton Koelb and Susan Noakes, 1988, p. 105.

17 See *Antiquity*, 15.11.400.

18 Jeanne Addison Roberts, 'Marriage and divorce in 1613: Elizabeth Cary, Frances Howard, and others', *Textual Formations and Reformations*, ed. Laurie E. Maguire and Thomas L. Berger, 1998, p. 162.

19 *ODNB, sub.* Penelope Rich.

divorce must have been of interest to the Cary family who resided in the parish when they were in London (see below). There was clearly a connection between the families because Henry Cary's nephew later married Sir Robert's grand-daughter. It is possible, therefore, that aspects of Elizabeth Cary's story were influenced by the Rich divorce. Penelope Rich, for example, was connected to the Sidneys through her brother, Essex, who had married Sir Philip Sidney's widow (and she was also, reputedly, the 'Stella' of Sidney's famous sonnets). Cary's choice of the closet drama form, closely associated with the Sidney family, might have been more than a bid to associate herself with the Countess of Pembroke.

It has long been noted that Cary's Mariam is presented as a chaste foil to Cleopatra, and that Cleopatra is portrayed sympathetically in Pembroke's translation. Cary's choice of genre and the allusions to Cleopatra connect Mariam with Pembroke's Antonius, and, by extension, to the Sidney family. In the context of the Devereux/Rich divorce, Mariam appears to invoke, but also subtly oppose, the Countess of Pembroke's play. At face value, this might indicate sympathy for Sir Robert Rich through its condemnation of unruly, Cleopatra-like women, yet, despite its choric assertions about women's proper submission to their husbands, the play's position on female subordination is not clear: Mariam's rejection of the marital bed turns her into a martyr, and the unruly Salome goes unpunished. As with her play's adoption and transformation of Petrarchan poetic forms, Cary employs and transforms motifs from Sidnean closet drama at a time when her clientage ties perhaps opposed her to the Devereux/Sidney family. That said, it is a bizarre coincidence that her own divorce – from the Protestant church – took place on 14 November 1626, the twenty-first anniversary of the dissolution of the Devereux/Rich marriage.[20]

In 1613, the Carys were on the margins of another divorce when Lady Frances Devereux (née Howard) sought the annulment of her marriage to Robert, second Earl of Essex. Rumours about an annulment were circulating in London at least a year before the legal process began in May 1613, and several plays dealing with divorce were published or reprinted in 1613. Henry Cary and Frances Howard were second cousins and the former would be invited, in January 1614, to tilt in a masque to celebrate the latter's remarriage to Robert Carr, Earl of Somerset. Given this family connection, it is interesting to wonder whether Cary's manuscript of Mariam, with its figure of the adulterous Salome, became newly interesting to the Cary family at this time and led, perhaps, to its publication.

20 For the date of Cary's conversion, see Wolfe, p. xvi.

Tyranny

The image of marriage was often used in the early modern period to figure the union between a monarch and the state, and was particularly prevalent during the reign of James I. For example, in one of the king's early speeches to parliament he asserted that he was the nation's husband and 'all the whole isle' was his 'lawful wife'.[21] The image of the family became a metaphor for statecraft and could be used by writers who wanted to investigate the methods and abuses of monarchical rule.

Cary's interest in monarchical absolutism is clear in her texts of *Edward II*, and her best work was reputed to be a life of Tamberlaine, the tyrannous Parthian emperor.[22] *Mariam* – written probably in the aftermath of the 1605 Gunpowder Plot that attempted to assassinate England's king – deals, in Diane Purkiss's words, with the question: 'when does it become lawful for the subject to resist?'.[23] The first two acts of the play take place in a hiatus of authority, with Herod absent in Rome and presumed dead. This hiatus is filled with the competing voices of women as Mariam, Alexandra and Salome struggle with each other for social supremacy. However, it is also a space in which political disobedience comes to light as Constabarus is revealed to have been protecting the sons of Baba against Herod's will and Pheroras disobeys his royal brother's instructions about his marriage.

In this play obsessed with social hierarchy and blood lines, clientage ties and influence derived from proximity to power are very noticeable. Constabarus and Baba's sons are linked by mutual obligation; Alexandra exhorts Mariam to remember her filial debts to her late relations; and Salome intercedes with Herod for Pheroras. The dangers of this type of system are made apparent as Salome's voice in Herod's ear leads to the condemnation and death of her husband, Baba's sons, Sohemus, and Herod's own wife. At once figuring the trouble that ensues when a woman is permitted to meddle in statecraft, the play also presents Herod as an autocratic, imperceptive and tyrannous king, who is manipulated by bad advisers: explicitly, his sister (a woman) and the butler (his social inferior).

Mariam's opening speech, while drawing on the conventional notion that women are inconstant, places the blame for that inconstancy on Herod whose jealousy has driven out Mariam's love (I.i.23–6). Herod is shown as a flawed king and vacillator who cannot even decide how to kill his wife. He is also an oath-breaker: Doris castigates him for breaking his

21 James I, 'A speech as it was delivered in the upper house of the Parliament', *King James VI and I: Political Writings*, ed. Johann P. Sommerville, 1994, p. 136.
22 Wolfe, p. 110.
23 Purkiss, p. xxxiv.

promises to her (II.iii.25–8), while, in constrast, Constabarus remains true to his oath that he will not fight for Salome (II.iv.8) and Mariam maintains her vow that she will never again share her bed with her husband (III.iii.16).

The *Life* notes that Elizabeth Cary took oaths very seriously and perjury and oathbreaking are certainly strong features of her *Edward II* which is at pains to explain:

> The eye of the world may be blinded, and the severity of human conditions removed; but ... perjury seldom escapes unpunished by the Divine Justice, who admits no dalliance with oaths, even in the case of necessity.[24]

In Cary's play, Mariam refuses to compromise her personal integrity for the purposes of outward show, scorning her 'look should ever man beguile' (III.iii.47). The play indicates that survival in the world of the court depends upon moral flexibility and deception, but, in its depiction of Mariam's death as a kind of martyrdom, presents her constancy to her vow in a positive light, and, in the process, locates Herod as an unsteadfast, dangerous tyrant who has broken his vows to Doris. The play seems to place personal conscience over obedience to the secular powers, not only in the case of Mariam, but also in that of Constabarus. At the other end of the spectrum, however, such disregard for secular authority (brought about, it seems, by Herod's failings as a ruler) leads Salome to consider breaking both her marriage oaths and the law that says only men are permitted to divorce. In sum, making use of imagery that allies the structure of the family with that of the nation, the play demonstrates that Herod's absence, and then his personal inadequacies, lead to political, social and personal disruption that endangers not only his immediate relatives but also the integrity of the state.

Catholicism, judgement, and truth

The notion of oath-breaking was forcefully under debate in 1606 when, in the aftermath of the Gunpowder Plot, James I introduced the oath of allegiance which asserted he was the rightful king of the realm and that no authority had the right to depose him. His Catholic subjects were required to swear that no power could absolve them of their oath, and that it was made 'without any equivocation, or mental evasion, or secret

---

24 *The History of . . . King Edward II*, 1680, 8°, pp. 15–16. For Cary's view of oaths, see Wolfe, p. 114.

reservation whatsoever'.[25] Because she had not yet declared her religious conversion, Cary was not directly affected by the crisis of conscience engendered by the oath. However, although it is clearly problematic to read the play as a Catholic's response to this conflict, it is less so to see it as engaging with the topical issues of equivocation, oath-taking and deception.

Indeed, Margaret Ferguson suggests that the play makes a topical allusion to the Gunpowder Plot when Salome accuses Mariam of having a heart as 'false as powder' (IV.vii.74). Salome, she says, paints Mariam as a scheming wife, her image yoking together the idea of powder as an explosive and as 'a cosmetic hiding something from the eye' and opening up the possibility that Mariam's own assertions of chastity and honesty are equivocal.[26] In other words, the multiple perspectives the play affords us of its various characters lead us to wonder who, if anyone, is telling the truth even when, like Mariam, they claim that is exactly what they are doing.

The play is, from the first, a disquisition on the nature of truth, language, and the conflict between inner thoughts and outward show. Constabarus, speaking with Baba's sons, shows himself to recognise the problems of hearing and reception: 'If any word of mine your heart did grieve,' he says, 'The word dissented from the speaker's will' (II.ii.77–8). Similarly, despite Salome's assertions to the contrary, Mariam is at pains to explain that her outside and inside reflect the same emotions: 'I cannot frame disguise, nor never taught / My face a look dissenting from my thought' (IV.iii.58–9), she says, in a scene that seems deliberately to allude to Hamlet's assertion that he 'is' and does not know how to 'seem' (I.ii.76).

It is often noted that Cary presented her eldest daughter with a ring upon which was inscribed the phrase: 'Be and seem'.[27] At face value, this seems to advocate sentiments similar to those expressed both by Mariam and Hamlet, disavowing deception and upholding a continuity between inner thoughts and outward show. Nevertheless, as Alexandra Bennet notes, the 'possibility of a deliberate discrepancy between [Mariam's] inner and outer selves is always in the background of her actions',[28] and we are reminded of an analogous sentiment in Othello, 'men should be what they seem' (III.iii.132), uttered by the Machiavellian Iago as he consummately pretends to be other than he is. The Life maintains that Cary

---

25For further information about the oath, see W. B. Patterson, King James VI and I and the Reunion of Christendom, 1997, pp. 80ff.

26 Margaret W. Ferguson, Dido's Daughters: Literacy, Gender, and Empire in Early Modern England and France, 2003, p. 301.

27 Wolfe, p. 118.

28 Alexandra G. Bennet, 'Female performativity in The Tragedy of Mariam', Studies in English Literature, 1500–1900 40.2 (2000), p. 300.

advised her eldest daughter on her marriage 'that wheresoever conscience and reason would permit her, she should prefer the will of another before her own'.[29] Ostensibly advocating complete obedience, the qualifying phrase 'wheresoever conscience and reason would permit', provides room for equivocation and mental reservation, just as Cary's play, in Bennet's words, reveals 'a remarkable awareness of the possibilities afforded to women by different tactics of self-representation'.[30]

In the end, in the face of deceit and possible equivocation, what the play advocates is the exercise of judgement, the subject of the second chorus. William Hamlin has noted that Cary was 'intrigued by the complex epistemological relations among knowing, perceiving, seeming, and believing', observing that the play draws on Montaigne's ideas about reason and feeling as it teaches its audience to 'become active participants in an ongoing dialectic of judicial assessment'.[31] In a mutable world, full of 'human error' (Chorus II.119), the play maintains that 'no content attends a wavering mind' (Chorus I.124), and advocates caution before taking decisions, suggesting we should 'try before we trust' (Chorus II.122; V.i.109). The play debates the problems involved in distinguishing between truth and untruth, and, even at the same time as it makes evident the possibility of equivocation, advocates one should remain true to one's oath, whatever that oath may be.

At the end of the play, *Mariam*'s final chorus concludes: 'This day's events were certainly ordained / To be the warning to posterity' (Chorus V. 289–90). Twenty years later, Cary's history of *Edward II* would close similarly, with the words:

[Edward's] doom was registered by that inscrutable providence of Heaven, who with the self-same sentence punished both him and Richard the Second his great grandchild, who were guilty of the same offences. The example of these two so unfortunate kings may be justly a leading precedent to all posterity.[32]

Participating in a discourse that reads history as an expression of a divine plan, *Mariam* is not just concerned with the splitting and fragmentation of the female subject within a society that tries to exercise control over a woman's body and mind, but with the intrinsic instability of the fallen,

29 Wolfe, p. 115.
30 Bennet, p. 298.
31 William M. Hamlin, 'Elizabeth Cary's *Mariam* and the critique of pure reason', *Early Modern Literary Studies* 9.1 (2003), electronic resource (accessed July 2009), pgh. 2.
32 *Edward II*, 8°, p. 74.

mortal world where deceit can be taken for truth and insides are rarely coterminous with outsides. Beneath it all, perhaps, is the truth of God's providence. Yet, despite its presentation of Mariam as a proto-Christ-like martyr, what the play leaves us with, ultimately, is a radical disquisition on the nature of appearances, deception and doubt.

The Author

The 1613 edition of *Mariam* identifies the play's author as 'E. C.', while its dedicatory sonnet mentions the author's 'worthy sister, Mistress Elizabeth Cary'. These clues have led to the belief that the play was written by Elizabeth Cary, wife of Sir Henry Cary, Viscount Falkland. She was born in 1585 at Burford Priory in Oxfordshire, and was the daughter of Sir Lawrence Tanfield (a lawyer, MP and, in 1607, chief baron of the exchequer) and his wife Elizabeth (née Symondes).

According to a biographical *Life*, written by one of her daughters, the young Elizabeth Tanfield 'learned to read very soon and loved it much' and also learned French, Spanish, Italian, Latin, Hebrew and Transylvanian 'without a teacher' or 'with very little teaching'.[33] Despite this claim, it is possible she benefitted from the tuition of poet and historian Michael Drayton, who dedicated two epistles of his *England's Heroical Epistles* to her when she was about eleven or twelve years old. It also seems she was taught by Sir John Davies of Hereford: he terms her his 'Pupil' in dedicatory verses to his *Muse's Sacrifice* (1612). As a childhood exercise, she translated an abridged edition of Abraham Ortelius's cartographical treatise, the *Miroir du monde*, out of French, dedicating her manuscript to her great uncle, Henry Lee, Queen Elizabeth I's champion and nephew of the Elizabethan sonneteer, Sir Thomas Wyatt. The *Life* explains she also translated Seneca's *Epistles* out of Latin.[34] An only child and her father's heir, Elizabeth benefitted from an education actively supported by her family, and tried to put this into use after her marriage to help advance her husband's career.

She was married in October 1602 to Sir Henry Cary, son of Sir Edward Cary and Catherine (née Knyvett). Henry travelled to the Low Countries in 1604, leaving his wife with his mother at Aldenham and Berkhamstead in Hertfordshire, and did not return to England until 1606 because he was captured and held prisoner in Spain until his family raised a ransom. It was around this time that Elizabeth Cary wrote a text about Syracuse in Sicily, dedicated to her husband. After his return, she may have accompanied Sir Henry to court, and shortly afterwards the couple began

33 Wolfe, pp. 105–6.
34 Wolfe, p. 106.

to have children. Their daughter Katherine was born in 1609, and Cary carried another ten children to term, baptising the last, Henry, in 1625. In April 1613, when she was about four months pregnant with her son Lorenzo, her husband danced in Thomas Campion's entertainment for Queen Anne at Caversham, Berkshire, and on 1 January 1614, before she conceived her daughter Anne, he tilted in Ben Jonson's masque for the marriage of Robert Carr, Earl of Somerset, and Frances Howard. Elizabeth Cary may have attended one or both of these entertainments. Both her children, though, were baptised at Berkhamstead, so it seems likely her main residence was there.

When in London, the Cary family lived in the parish of St Bartholomew-the-Great: Henry Cary lived next door to his sister Jane and her husband Edward Barrett.[35] (It was this sister-in-law upon whom Elizabeth Cary relied during the early years of her recusancy when her husband tried to banish her from London.) Henry Cary baptised two children in the parish, in 1617 and 1619, and it seems clear that he frequently visited London, particularly after 1617 when he became comptroller of the King's household and a member of his privy council.[36] Indeed, the *Life* notes that, from this point on, Elizabeth Cary 'came to live frequently at his lodgings at court', although, from the baptismal records, it seems more likely she resided in St Bartholomew's.[37]

Despite his court position, Henry Cary suffered financial troubles and, in October 1622, it was rumoured he was so far in debt he should leave England and procure a place in Ireland.[38] Sure enough, in May 1622, he was appointed Lord Deputy of Ireland and mortgaged his wife's jointure to fund his appointment. William Basse, an Oxfordshire poet, wrote two poems on 'Lady Falkland's Going to Ireland' at this time, invoking Cary's Muse and asserting that praise of her had gone before her to Ireland.[39] This notion of her as a literary patron is borne out by a subsequent dedication from an Irish writer, Richard Bellings, who dedicated his continuation of *The Countess of Pembroke's Arcadia* to her in 1624. His dedication implies that the work was written at her instigation, demonstrating, at the very least, that her learning and literary interests were known in Ireland as well as England.

In 1625, Elizabeth Cary returned to London with four of her children and proceeded immediately to court where she worked hard to promote

35 E. A. Webb, *The records of St. Bartholomew's priory [and] St. Bartholomew the Great*, 2 vols., 1921, II, p. 269.
36 *ODNB*, *sub*. Henry Cary.
37 Wolfe, p. 119.
38 Wolfe, p. 226.
39 William Basse, 'Polyhymnia', Chetham's Library, Manchester, MS A.3.54, 9r–v.

her husband's career.[40] Henry Cary was, however, unconvinced by his wife's political abilities, observing that he did 'conceive women to be no fit solicitors of state affairs, for though it sometimes happen that they have good wits, it then commonly falls out that they have over-busy natures withal'.[41] After the public declaration of Elizabeth's conversion to Catholicism, he wrote to King Charles to declare he had 'long unhappily' called her his wife.[42] Charles confined her to her house for six weeks and Henry cut off all financial support, but she refused to recant her Catholic faith.

The *Life* informs us that Cary began to doubt her religion after reading Hooker's *Ecclesiastical Polity* when she was about twenty years old (around three years after her marriage). This Protestant book 'left her hanging in the air' and she could not see 'how, nor at what, she could stop, till she returned to the church from whence they were come'. Her feelings about Catholicism were confirmed by Adolphus Cary, her brother-in-law, who returned from Italy with 'a good opinion of catholic religion' and encouraged her to read the Church Fathers, especially St Augustine. This increased her suspicion of Protestantism, but she persuaded herself at first that she 'might lawfully remain as she was'. Indeed, the *Life* states that she stayed a Protestant another twenty-two years, 'flattering herself with good intentions', before her final conversion on 14 November 1626.[43]

The years after Cary's conversion were ones of hardship, but it was during this time that she wrote, and then expanded, a prose history of *Edward II*. She survived on money lent by various benefactors, including the Viscountess Mountgarret, wife of Henry Cary's political enemy, Richard Butler.[44] Henry was ordered by the Privy Council to provide her with a pension, but defaulted on payments and she was still petitioning the King for help in April 1630.[45] It was during this year that she translated Cardinal du Perron's *Replique à la response du sérénisime roy de la grande-bretagne* (1620), part of a controversial religious debate between King James I and the papacy. Cary's translation was published in France and is unashamed in its promotion of its author's abilities. 'I will not make use of that worn-out form of saying I printed it against my will, moved by the importunity of friends', Cary says in an address to the

40 Wolfe, p. 125.
41 Wolfe, p. 256.
42 Wolfe, p. 268.
43 Wolfe, pp. 110–12.
44 *Calendar of State Papers, Ireland, 1625–32*, p. 279. See also *ODNB*, *sub*. Richard Butler.
45 *Calendar of State Papers, Domestic, 1629–31*, p. 233.

reader, continuing, 'I was moved to it by my belief that it might make those English that understand not French, whereof there are many even in our universities, read Perron'.[46] Notably, Cary dedicated her translation to Charles I's French Catholic Queen Henrietta Maria.

The *Life* asserts that a reconciliation between Elizabeth and Henry Cary was finally brokered by Henrietta Maria, who was clearly taking an interest in their family.[47] In 1632, their daughter, Victoria, danced in the Queen's masque, *Tempe Restored*, and then performed the male, speaking role of Martiro in the Queen's court play, *The Shepherds' Paradise*. This play caused a minor furore because it coincided with the publication of *Histriomastix*, a polemical opus by the Protestant lawyer, William Prynne, which declared that women actors were 'notorious whores'. Prynne was prosecuted and several publishers and playwrights rallied to defend the theatre. It was in this climate that Elizabeth Cary received her final printed dedication, from William Sheares, the publisher of John Marston's *Works* (1633), who castigated the anti-theatricalists and declared that Cary was the admiration 'not only of this island, but of all adjacent countries and dominions'. During this time, Cary also wrote lives of the saints Mary Magdalen, Agnes the Martyr and Elizabeth of Portugal, plus several poems to the Virgin.[48] She then began to translate the Latin work of the Flemish mystic, Louis de Blois. This translation was left unfinished on her death.

Cary died in 1639, six years after her husband, and was buried in London in Henrietta Maria's Catholic chapel. At her death, she had managed to arrange the religious conversions of six of her children and her faithful servant, Bessie Poulter. All four of her Catholic daughters became nuns in France: her two Catholic sons entered religious orders, but later recanted, returning to England and taking up the law.

Performance History

One of the most often quoted passages about Elizabeth Cary from the *Life* reads: 'After her lord's death she never went to masques nor plays not so much as at the court, though she loved them very much, especially the last extremely'.[49] It is impossible to know what early exposure Elizabeth Cary had to the theatre, but it is likely that, at the very least, she either saw or read the *Lord Hay's Masque* in 1607 (see 'Date' section above). What is certain, is that *Mariam* has proved to be an eminently performable play.

46 Elizabeth Cary, *The Reply of the Most Illustrious Cardinall of Perron*, 1630, sig. a2v.
47 Wolfe, p. 145.
48 Wolfe, p. 141.
49 Wolfe, pp. 155–6.

Nonetheless, even though early writers clearly knew about it (Edward Phillips, for example, mentioned it in 1675), there is no evidence *Mariam* was performed in the seventeenth century.[50] Indeed, it apparently did not receive its first full performance until 1994 at the Alhambra Studio in Bradford, Yorkshire, in a production directed by Stephanie Hodgson-Wright. A year later, directed by Elizabeth Schafer, it was performed at Royal Holloway, London. In 1996, Paul Stephen Lim directed a staged reading at the University of Kansas, and it figured in another staged reading in 2007 as part of the Primavera Theatre Company's 'Forgotten Classics' series at the King's Head Theatre, Islington.

Rehearsals for Hodgson-Wright's production highlighted two intrinsically dramatic moments in the play: the sword fight in II.iii; and the moment in IV.iv where the butler brings Herod a cup of wine, resulting in a scene that 'revolves around a physical stage property'.[51] The play, Hodgson-Wright suggests, provides a forceful sense of physical relationships between its characters (who are constantly looking at each other) and between the characters and their surroundings. Consequently, her stage emphasised the play's spatial qualities as well as its concerns with tyranny: on the right was 'an area of imperialistic celebration' decorated with busts of Octavius Caesar, Mark Antony and Julius Caesar; on the left was a graveyard containing the bodies of Hircanus and Aristobolus. Stage centre was a 'defaced poster of Herod, figured as a petty dictator supported by a world super-power', and the whole was designed to oppose 'the celebration of political power with its bloody consequences'. The choice of modern dress for the actors helped to underline the contemporary significance of a play which also drew on modern theories of the gaze to present a world liberated from Herod's view and to dramatise the consequences of his return.[52]

Elizabeth Schafer's production used an all-female cast (with the exception of Antipater who was played by a boy). Her play used period costumes, largely inspired by the play's setting in Judea, and, like Wright's production, positioned Mariam (who also took the role of the Chorus) in front of a portrait of her husband. Again like Wright's production, it made use of modern critical ideas, this time by having Mariam read the misogynistic sentiments of the third chorus from a conduct book.[53]

Lim's staged reading cut the Baba's sons plot, but created a stronger comparison between the position of Mariam and Doris by placing

50 Edward Phillips, *Theatrum Poetarum*, 1675, p. 257.
51 Stephanie J. Hodgson-Wright, *et al.*, '"The play is ready to be acted": women and dramatic production, 1570–1670', *Women's Writing* 6.1 (1999), p. 133.
52 Hodgson-Wright (1999), p. 133.
53 Stephanie Hodgson-Wright, ed., *The Tragedy of Mariam*, 2000, p. 31.

Mariam's son on stage and contrasting him with Doris's Antipater.[54] The production thereby concentrated *Mariam*'s focus on women's roles, but reduced the play's wider political resonances. In contrast, the staged reading performed with a professional cast by the Primavera theatre company emphasised the extent to which 'The conflict between Mariam, descendant of the rightful Jewish ruler, and Herod, her Roman-appointed husband, resonates powerfully in the charged atmosphere of the Middle East today'.[55]

Wright makes a forceful point when she remarks that 'empirically speaking, *The Tragedy of Mariam* must, of necessity, be a performance text because it can, and has been, performed'.[56] That said, and despite all its performative elements, I suggest it was written to be read and not acted. A play with a significant subplot about divorce, written in the early 1600s when first Robert Rich and then Robert Devereux were involved in ending their marriages, was hot property. When one adds the clientage ties between the Cary family and Robert Rich, the idea of a performance of Mariam seems highly inflammatory, while the circulation of the text among a group of people interested in, and concerned by, his divorce seems much more likely.

A Note on the Text

There is only one early modern edition of the play, the 1613 quarto published by Richard Hawkins and printed by Thomas Creede. It bears Creede's ornament on its title page, and is made up of nine gatherings, signed A to I. The play ends on I2r. In two copies, now at the Houghton and Huntington libraries, A1r is present and contains the dedicatory verses, 'To my worthy sister', while 'The names of the speakers' are printed on the verso. This leaf was removed in other copies for stubs can be seen in quartos at Eton and the Bodleian Library. Scholars have connected the leaf's removal with the comment in the *Life* that Cary had one of her works called in.[57]

Creede's printers had experience of setting plays. However, *Mariam* contains several errors. On B1v, Mariam's speech is headed: '*Nun:*'; C1r has 'Waters-bearing' instead of 'water-bearing'; C2r has the uncorrected 'chreeful'; C4r has 'operpast' for 'overpast'; a speech heading is missing for Mariam at the bottom of E2r; 'hypcorite' is uncorrected on E2v; 'love' is printed 'boue' on F3v; and on F4r, 'causeless' is rendered 'caules'. However,

54 Hodgson-Wright, 2000, p. 32.
55 Primavera Productions website: (accessed July 2009).
56 Hodgson-Wright (1999), p. 136.
57 Wolfe, p. 110.

despite these errors, it is clear the play was corrected as it went through the press. There are four substantive changes: the catchword on G1v reads 'Youlle' in some copies and 'Youl'e' in others; some copies of G3v read 'a new' and some 'anew'; some versions of H4v carry the reading 'fame' (V.i.211, 213), while some read 'faine'. Weller and Ferguson also note that a copy in Edinburgh contains a unique variant on F3r; an 'I' which 'apparently fell out of the form . . . before the other extant copies were printed'.[58]

Mariam was one of the first books published by Hawkins after he set up business on his own in Chancery Lane. In his first year of publishing under his own name, he produced three volumes: Cary's Mariam (printed by Creede); Gervase Markham's Hobson's Horse-Load of Letters (printed by Thomas Snodham); and I. C.'s Alcilia Philoparthens loving folly (a miscellaneous collection of verses, printed by Snodham and Creede). It is surprising that he chose, or was chosen, to publish Mariam at this time, and that he agreed to produce a play by an unknown author. However, it is possible that Sir John Davies of Hereford was involved in negotiating the play's publication. Davies admired Cary and, in 1612, he lived in Fleet Street, near Chancery Lane.[59]

Mariam's publication has often been linked with the Life's observation that one of Cary's works was 'stolen out of that sister-in-law's (her friend's) chamber, and printed, but by her own procurement was called in'.[60] This statement may be a modest apology on the part of Cary's Catholic daughter for the play's publication, yet it does have some basis in fact. In 1607, Elizabeth Cary's sister-in-law, Anne Cary, married Sir Francis Leeke, who became Baron Deyncourt in 1624 and Earl of Scarsdale in 1645. Leeke was first cousins with Gervase Markham, through Markham's mother, Mary, daughter of Sir Francis Leeke and Elizabeth Patton. Both Cary's and Markham's books were published by Hawkins in 1613, and it seems likely that Mariam reached the print shop through Markham, via one of Cary's sisters-in-law. This does not, however, foreclose the possibility that Cary wished to publish her play and invoked the help of Markham, Sir John Davies, or both.

Cary certainly had a relationship with the Fleet Street and Chancery Lane publishers. In 1614, the bookseller Richard More, whose shop was in St Dunstan's churchyard, adjacent to Chancery Lane, dedicated an edition of John Bodenham's England's Helicon to her, calling her 'England's

58 Weller and Ferguson, p. 47.
59 See his will (1618) for evidence of his residence in Fleet Street: National Archives, PROB/11/132, fol. 97r–v.
60 Wolfe, p. 110.

happy Muse' and 'Learning's delight'. In 1633, she was the dedicatee of William Sheares's edition of *The Works of John Marston*. That year, Sheares also published Markham's play, *The Dumb Knight*, advertised 'to be sold at his shop in Chancery Lane'.[61] In other words, before dedicating their publications to her, both More and Sheares may have met Cary in their shops (which were about ten minutes walk from her London residences at St Bartholomew's and, later, Drury Lane). In addition, both Hawkins and Sheares had connections with Markham.

There is also indirect evidence that Markham knew *Mariam*. In 1613, in a dedicatory epistle to his continuation of Sidney's *Arcadia*, he made oblique reference to his '*Herodias*', possibly an early version of *Herod and Antipater* (1622), a play he co-authored with William Sampson. Although *Herod and Antipater* is very different from *Mariam*, some of its early scenes bear comparison, and it is possible Markham borrowed the manuscript of *Mariam* when he was writing *Herodias*, or perhaps was inspired to write his play after reading *Mariam*.[62] He was related to Elizabeth Cary through her sister-in-law and, in 1613, had connections with Hawkins who was clearly looking for publishable material as he began his business. It seems likely that Markham facilitated the play's publication, notably at a time when the issue of divorce was topical. The extent to which Cary was complicit in the play's publication may never be known.

In recent years, *Mariam* has received a lot of scholarly attention. This edition is indebted to Barry Weller and Margaret Ferguson's work, *The Tragedy of Mariam* (1994). It also makes use of Dunstan and Greg's 1914 Malone Society edition, Stephanie Hodgson-Wright's 2000 edition, Diane Purkiss's old-spelling text in *Three Tragedies by Renaissance Women* (1998), and Clare Carroll's 2002 version (printed with the text of *Othello*).

Spelling and punctuation are modernised here and the 1613 quarto's misprints corrected. Abbreviated names in the text are silently expanded and speech prefixes regularised. Additional stage directions are provided in square brackets.

---

61 Sheares moved shop between 1631–3 from St Paul's Yard to Britain's Burse, but seems to have worked briefly out of Chancery Lane.

62 Markham's II.i has a strikingly similar dramatic impact to I.iii in *Mariam* where Mariam, Alexandra and Salome declare their mutual antipathy. Equally, the scenes of Mariam's reported execution have a similar structure, even down to the emphasis on the quasi-saintly manner in which Mariam is reputed to have died.

ABBREVIATIONS

Ant.	Josephus, *Antiquity of the Jews*, in *The Famous and Memorable Works of Josephus*, trans. Thomas Lodge (1602)
Bell	Ilona Bell, 'Private lyrics in Elizabeth Cary's *Mariam*', *The Literary Career and Legacy of Elizabeth Cary, 1613–1680*, ed. Heather Wolfe (2007), pp. 17–34
Carroll	Clare Carroll, ed., *Othello and The Tragedy of Mariam* (2003)
Dunstan and Greg	A. C. Dunstan and W. W. Greg, eds, *The Tragedy of Mariam* (1914)
ed.	editor
Hodgson–Wright	Stephanie Hodgson-Wright, ed., *The Tragedy of Mariam* (2000)
Montaigne, *Essays*	Michel Montaigne, *The Essays*, trans. John Florio (1603)
n.s.	new series
ODNB	*Oxford Dictionary of National Biography*
OED	*Oxford English Dictionary*
Purkiss	Diane Purkiss, ed., *Three Tragedies by Renaissance Women* (1998)
Q	*The Tragedy of Mariam*, 1613 quarto
s.d.	stage direction
s.p.	speech prefix
Tilley	M. P. Tilley, *A Dictionary of the Proverbs in England in the Sixteenth and Seventeenth Centuries* (1950)
Wars	Josephus, *Seven Books of the Wars of the Jews* in *The Famous and Memorable Works of Josephus*, trans. Thomas Lodge (1602)
Weller and Ferguson	Barry Weller and Margaret Ferguson, eds, *The Tragedy of Mariam* (1994)
Wolfe	Heather Wolfe, ed., *Elizabeth Cary, Lady Falkland: Life and Letters* (2001)

All Shakespeare references are to *The Norton Shakespeare*, 2nd edn (2008)
All biblical references are to the Geneva Bible (1560)

FURTHER READING

Barish, Jonas, 'Language for the study, language for the stage', in *The Elizabethan Theatre XII*, ed. A. L. Magnusson and C. E. McGee, 1993, pp. 19–43.

Bennet, Alexandra G., 'Female performativity in *The Tragedy of Mariam*', *Studies in English Literature, 1500–1900* 40.2 (2000), 293–309.

Callaghan, Dympna, 'Re-reading Elizabeth Cary's *The Tragedie of Mariam, Faire Queene of Jewry*', in *Women, 'Race,' and Writing in the Early Modern Period*, ed. Margo Hendricks and Patricia Parker, 1994, pp. 163–77.

Ferguson, Margaret W., *Dido's Daughters: Literacy, Gender, and Empire in Early Modern England and France*, 2003.

————, 'A room not their own', in *The Comparative Perspective on Literature*, ed. Clayton Koelb and Susan Noakes, 1988, pp. 93–116.

Fischer, Sandra K., 'Elizabeth Cary and tyranny, domestic and religious', in *Silent but for the Word: Tudor Women as Patrons, Translators, and Writers of Religious Works*, ed. Margaret Patterson Hannay, 1985, pp. 225–37.

Goldberg, Jonathan, *Desiring Women Writing*, 1997.

Green, Reina, '"Ears prejudicate" in *Mariam* and *The Duchess of Malfi*', *Studies in English Literature, 1500–1900* 43.2 (2003), 459–74.

Hamlin, William M., 'Elizabeth Cary's *Mariam* and the critique of pure reason', *Early Modern Literary Studies* 9.1 (2003). (Electronic resource: http://purl.oclc.org/emls/09-1/hamlcary.html.)

Hiscock, Andrew, 'The hateful cuckoo: Elizabeth Cary's *Tragedie of Mariam*, a Renaissance drama of dispossession', *Forum for Modern Language Studies* 33.2 (1997), 97–114.

Hodgson-Wright, Stephanie J., *et al.*, '"The play is ready to be acted": women and dramatic production, 1570–1670', *Women's Writing* 6.1 (1999), 129–48.

Kelly, Erin E., '*Mariam* and early modern discourses of martyrdom', in *The Literary Career and Legacy of Elizabeth Cary, 1613–1680*, ed. Heather Wolfe, 2007, pp. 35–52.

Lewalski, Barbara, *Writing Women in Jacobean England*, 1993.

Miller, Naomi J., 'Domestic politics in Elizabeth Cary's *The Tragedy of Mariam*', *Studies in English Literature, 1500–1900* 37.2 (1997), 353–69.

Purkiss, Diane, 'Blood, sacrifice, marriage: why Iphigeneia and Mariam have to die', *Women's Writing* 6.1 (1999), 27–45.

Raber, Karen, 'Gender and the political subject in the *Tragedy of Mariam*', *Studies in English Literature, 1500–1900* 35.2 (1995), 321–43.

————, *Ashgate Critical Essays on Women Writers in England, 1550–1700: volume 6 Elizabeth Cary*, 2009.

————, *Dramatic Difference: Gender, Class, and Genre in the Early Modern Closet Drama*, 2001.

Richardson, Peter, *Herod: King of the Jews and Friend of the Romans*, 1996.

Roberts, Jeanne Addison, 'Marriage and divorce in 1613: Elizabeth Cary, Frances Howard, and others', in *Textual Formations and Reformations*, ed. Laurie E. Maguire and Thomas L. Berger, 1998, pp. 161–78.

Shell, Alison, 'Elizabeth Cary's historical conscience', *The Literary Career and Legacy of Elizabeth Cary, 1613–1680*, ed. Heather Wolfe, 2007, pp. 53–67.

Skura, Meredith, 'The reproduction of mothering in *Mariam, Queen of Jewry*: a defense of "biographical" criticism', *Tulsa Studies in Women's Literature* 16.1 (1997), 27–56.

Straznicky, Marta, *Privacy, Playreading, and Women's Closet Drama, 1550–1700*, 2004.

Travitsky, Betty, 'The *Feme Covert* in Elizabeth Cary's *Mariam*', in *Ambiguous Realities: Women in the Middle Ages and Renaissance*, ed. Carole Levin and Jeanie Watson, 1987, pp. 184–96.

Zimmerman, Shari A., 'Disaffection, dissimulation, and the uncertain ground of silent dismission: juxtaposing John Milton and Elizabeth Cary', *English Literary History* 66 (1999), 553–89.

Opposite: facsimile title-page of the 1613 quarto,
reproduced by permission of the Huntington Library,
San Marino, California

THE TRAGEDIE

OF MARIAM,
THE FAIRE
Queene of Iewry.

Written by that learned,
vertuous, and truly noble Ladie,
E. C.

LONDON.

Printed by Thomas Creede, for Richard
Hawkins, and are to be solde at his shoppe
in Chancery Lane, neere vnto
Sargeants Inne.
1613.

DEDICATION

TO DIANA'S EARTHLY DEPUTESS,
and my worthy sister,
Mistress Elizabeth Cary.

When cheerful Phoebus his full course hath run,
His sister's fainter beams our hearts doth cheer:
So your fair brother is to me the sun,
And you, his sister, as my moon appear.

You are my next belov'd, my second friend,   5
For when my Phoebus' absence makes it night,
Whilst to th' antipodes his beams do bend,
From you, my Phoebe, shines my second light.

He like to Sol, clear-sighted, constant, free;
You Luna-like, unspotted, chaste, divine: 10
He shone on Sicily, you destined be
T'illumine the now-obscurèd Palestine.
My first was consecrated to Apollo;
My second to Diana now shall follow.

                         E. C.   15

---

0   *DIANA'S . . . DEPUTESS* Diana's representative on earth. Diana was the Roman goddess of chastity. Her emblem was the moon. (See ll. 8, 10 below.)
     sister . . . Cary Scholars have speculated that this Elizabeth Cary was Henry Cary's sister-in-law, Elizabeth Bland Cary (see Introduction for more details).

1–14   This dedicatory verse is a sonnet, the first of many throughout the play (see Bell,18, and Introduction).

1   *Phoebus* The Roman sun god who drove his chariot daily across the sky from east to west.

7   *th' antipodes* the other side of the globe. Richard Brome published a play called *The Antipodes* in 1640.

8, 10   *Phoebe, Luna* Alternative names for the moon goddess. (See note 0 above.)

9, 13   *Sol, Apollo* Alternative names for the sun god.

11   *He . . . Sicily* A previous work by Cary, dedicated to her husband, was reputedly set in Syracuse, south-east Sicily (see Introduction).

15   *E. C.* The play's author is identified only with these initials. Scholarly consensus suggests they refer to Elizabeth Cary, wife of Henry Cary (see Introduction).

THE NAMES OF THE SPEAKERS

HEROD, *King of Judea*
DORIS, *his first wife*
MARIAM, *his second wife*
SALOME, *Herod's sister*
ANTIPATER, *his son by Doris*   5
ALEXANDRA, *Mariam's mother*
SILLEUS, *Prince of Arabia*
CONSTABARUS, *husband to Salome*
PHERORAS, *Herod's brother*
GRAPHINA, *his love*   10
BABA'S FIRST SON
BABA'S SECOND SON
ANANELL, *the High Priest*
SOHEMUS, *a counsellor to Herod*
NUNTIO [*a messenger*]   15
BUTLER, *another messenger*
CHORUS, *a company of Jews*

1   HEROD King Herod the Great (73-4 BCE), son of Antipater, the Idumean. A number of texts, including the Bishops' Bible, present Herod's rule as the time when the Jews ceased to be God's chosen people and the way was cleared for the coming of Christ.

2   DORIS Josephus says she was of Herod's 'own nation' (*Ant.*, 14.21.368).

3   MARIAM A member of the Jewish Hasmonean dynasty, founded by Simon Maccabaeus in *c.* 142 BCE (see 1 Maccabees and 2 Maccabees). Her name evokes comparisons with the Virgin Mary and Miriam, sister of Moses, both models for a pious, female writer (see Shell, 58). She married Herod in 37 BCE.

4   SALOME Not to be confused with the Salome who demanded the head of John the Baptist, the adopted daughter of Herod Antipas, son of Herod the Great. Nevertheless, the taint of dangerous, female seductiveness stains both women.

5   *Doris* ed. (*Salome* Q).

6   ALEXANDRA A member of the Hasmonean dynasty. Josephus describes her as 'full of feminine pride' and 'desiring rather to suffer anything, than be deprived of the liberty of free speech' (*Ant.*, 15.3.385).

7   SILLEUS Described by Josephus as 'a crafty fellow' and 'very beautiful' (*Ant.*, 16.11.425).

8   CONSTABARUS Josephus says he was an Idumean and 'of the greatest account among his countrymen' (*Ant.*, 15.11.400).

10   GRAPHINA The name is unique to *Mariam*, although it might be inspired by the name 'Glaphyra', one of Pheroras's maids in Josephus (*Ant.*, 16.11.423-4).

11–12   BABA's ... SON Josephus mentions '*Babas* children' and '*Babas* sonnes', noting they had been in Constabarus's care for twelve years (*Ant.*, 15.11.400). Baba's sons were, like Mariam, members of the Hasmonean dynasty. Q alternates between the spellings '*Babus*' and '*Baba*'. '*Baba*' is preferred here.

13   ANANELL Described by Josephus as a Babylonian Jew of 'base condition' to whom the high priesthood was given by Herod (*Ant.*, 15.2.384; 15.3.385).

15   NUNTIO Messenger.

16   BUTLER ed. (*Bu.* Q).

5

THE ARGUMENT

Herod, the son of Antipater (an Idumean), having crept by the favour of the Romans into the Jewish monarchy, married Mariam, the daughter of Hircanus, the rightful king and priest, and for her (besides her high blood, being of singular beauty) he repudiated Doris, his former wife, by whom he had children.   5

This Mariam had a brother called Aristobolus, and next him and Hircanus, his grandfather, Herod, in his wife's right, had the best title. Therefore, to remove them, he charged the first with treason and put him to death, and drowned the second under colour of sport. Alexandra, daughter to the one, and mother to the other,   10
accused him for their deaths before Antony.

So when he was forced to go answer this accusation at Rome, he left the custody of his wife to Josephus, his uncle, that had married his sister, Salome, and out of a violent affection (unwilling any should enjoy her after him), he gave strict and private command-   15

1   *Antipater* The father of Herod, he was appointed procurator of Judea, Samaria and
     Galilee by Julius Caesar in 47 BCE. Josephus calls him 'a just and virtuous man'
     (*Ant.*, 14.19.367).
     Idumean The Idumeans (formerly the Edomites) came from the southern part of
     Judea and were descended from Esau, brother of Jacob. They were forced to con-
     vert to Judaism by John Hircanus, Mariam's great-great-grandfather, and were
     frequently regarded as only half Jews. See I.iii.29 below.
1–2 *crept . . . monarchy* Herod was maintained in his position by the patronage of the
     Roman leaders, Mark Antony and Octavian (see *Ant.*, 14.26.374).
3   *daughter* This can mean grand-daughter, as it does here. Mariam's maternal
     grandfather was Hircanus II. He was High Priest and sometime King of Judea.
     Antipater, Herod's father, was his adviser.
6   *Aristobolus* Aristobolus III, Mariam's eighteen-year-old brother. According to
     Josephus, Herod was coerced by Mariam's family into making him high priest, but
     arranged for him to be drowned after only one year in office (*Ant.*, 15.3.386).
7   *wife's right* Herod claimed the right to the throne through his wife's descent from
     the Hasmonean dynasty.
8   *he* Herod.
     the first Hircanus. Editors note that the logical, grammatical order here is reversed.
     However, arguably, Hircanus is called 'the first' because he is the most senior. (See
     Ant., 15.9.394, for an account of his death.)
     the second Aristobolus.
11   *Antony* Mark Antony. Josephus notes that Alexandra complained to Cleopatra
     about her son's death, and Cleopatra enlisted Antony, one of the triumvirate of
     Roman leaders, to avenge the child's murder (*Ant.*, 15.4.387).
13   *Josephus* See *Ant.*, 15.4.387, for a fuller account of this story.
15   *her* Mariam.

ment that, if he were slain, she should be put to death. But he
returned with much honour, yet found his wife extremely dis-
contented, to whom Josephus had (meaning it for the best, to
prove Herod loved her) revealed his charge.

So, by Salome's accusation, he put Josephus to death, but was   20
reconciled to Mariam who still bare the death of her friends
exceeding hardly.

In this meantime, Herod was again necessarily to revisit Rome,
for Caesar, having overthrown Antony, his great friend, was likely
to make an alteration of his fortune.   25

In his absence, news came to Jerusalem that Caesar had put
him to death. Their willingness it should be so, together with the
likelihood, gave this rumour so good credit as Sohemus, that had
succeeded Josephus' charge, succeeded him likewise in revealing it.
So at Herod's return, which was speedy and unexpected, he found   30
Mariam so far from joy that she showed apparent signs of sorrow.
He, still desiring to win her to a better humour, she, being very
unable to conceal her passion, fell to upbraiding him with her
brother's death. As they were thus debating, came in a fellow with
a cup of wine, who, hired by Salome, said first it was a love potion 35
which Mariam desired to deliver to the king, but afterwards he
affirmed that it was a poison, and that Sohemus had told her somewhat which procured the vehement hate in her.

The king hearing this, more moved with jealousy of Sohemus
than with this intent of poison, sent her away, and presently after   40
by the instigation of Salome she was beheaded. Which rashness
was afterward punished in him with an intolerable and almost
frantic passion for her death.

21   *bare* bore.
      friends relatives, but also, presumably, Josephus.
22   *exceeding hardly* very deeply. This line is a paraphrase of *Ant.*, 15.11.399: 'She
      digested also the loss of her friends very hardly'.
24   *Caesar* Octavius (or Augustus) Caesar.
      his Herod's.
29   *succeeded . . . charge* taken on Josephus's responsibilities (i.e. to guard Mariam).
37–8 *somewhat* something.

ACT I, SCENE i

[Enter] MARIAM *sola*

MARIAM   Foreverful

How oft have I with public voice run on
To censure Rome's last hero for deceit
Because he wept when Pompey's life was gone,
Yet, when he lived, he thought his name too great?
But now I do recant, and, Roman lord,   5
Excuse too rash a judgement in a woman:
My sex pleads pardon, pardon then afford,
Mistaking is with us but too, too common.
Now do I find, by self-experience taught,
One object yields both grief and joy: 10

---

   0   s.d. ed. (Actus primus. Scoena prima. Q).
        s.d. *sola* alone.
   1   Many critics remark that this line, with its personal pronoun and active verb,
        foregrounds Mariam's agency as a woman who will speak in public. However, the
        awareness that her voice has 'run on', coupled with her subsequent admission she
        was 'rash' (l. 6), indicates Mariam is aware she has lacked verbal restraint.
1–14 The play's first fourteen lines form a sonnet, which has been described as offering
        'a counterpoint to Renaissance literary convention' by foregrounding a female
        perspective (Bell, 19–20).
   2   *censure* criticise.
        Rome's last hero Julius Caesar. Despite her self-effacing apologies at ll. 5–8, it is
        notable that Mariam compares herself to a famous, male leader.
   3   *he . . . gone* Plutarch reports that Julius Caesar wept at Pompey's murder (Plutarch,
        Lives, 718). Pompey was a military leader and politician and, with Caesar and
        Marcus Licinius Crassus, made up the first Roman triumvirate.
   5   *now* 'Now' occurs eight times in this speech, perhaps drawing attention to the play's
        adherence to the classical unity of time (see Bell, 20, and Introduction).
        recant retract my former opinion.
        Roman lord Mariam directly addresses Caesar. The use of apostrophe will become
        one of the play's persistent rhetorical features. (For further examples in this scene,
        see I.i.43; 63; 67; 75.)
6–8   *Excuse . . . common* Mariam excuses herself by invoking popular ideas about
        women's intellectual frailty. The sophisticated rhetorical structure of her soliloquy
        – which, in l. 7, employs anadiplosis, i.e. repeating the last word of the clause at the
        beginning of the next – gives the lie to what she is saying.
 10 The line is metrically deficient in Q. A contemporary hand in the Huntington
        Library quarto supplies the word 'onely' between 'object' and 'yields'. This
        sentiment is indebted to Montaigne's *Essays*, 1.37, 'How we weep and laugh at one
        self-same thing'.

9

You wept indeed, when on his worth you thought,
But joyed that slaughter did your foe destroy.
So, at his death, your eyes true drops did rain,
Whom dead, you did not wish alive again.
When Herod lived, that now is done to death,   15
Oft have I wished that I from him were free,
Oft have I wished that he might lose his breath,
Oft have I wished his carcass dead to see.
Then rage and scorn had put my love to flight –
That love which once on him was firmly set –   20
Hate hid his true affection from my sight
And kept my heart from paying him his debt.
And blame me not, for Herod's jealousy
Had power even constancy itself to change,
For he, by barring me from liberty,   25
To shun my ranging, taught me first to range.
But yet too chaste a scholar was my heart
To learn to love another than my lord:
To leave his love, my lesson's former part,
I quickly learned. The other I abhorred.   30
But now his death to memory doth call
The tender love that he to Mariam bare,
And mine to him. This makes those rivers fall
Which by another thought unmoistened are.
For Aristobolus, the lowliest youth   35
That ever did in angel's shape appear,

16–18   *Oft . . . see* Cary employs the rhetorical device of anaphora – i.e. repeating the same
words at the start of a phrase – to emphasise how often Mariam has wished to be
rid of Herod. (For other examples of anaphora in the play, see I.vi.50–4; 64–8;
IV.vi.33–8; 50–6; IV.viii.23–6; 124–8; V.i.22–4.)

23–4   *Herod's jealousy . . . change* Herod's jealousy could turn his wife into an inconstant
woman.

26–30   The vocabulary of scholarship here ('taught', 'scholar', 'learn', 'lesson') plays
ironically on the biblical idea of the husband as the wife's teacher (see 1
Corinthians 14.35). Herod's actions taught Mariam to ignore his love for her, but
her intrinsic chastity made her detest adultery.

26   *shun* prevent (*OED*, *shun*, *v*. 4b).

27   *heart* ed. (hart Q). The connection with 'ranging' in l. 26 obliquely puns on 'hart'
as 'deer', comparing loving with hunting.

32   *bare* bore.

35   *lowliest* Dunstan and Greg suggest emending to 'loveliest' because of Josephus's
constant emphasis on Aristobolus's beauty. Weller and Ferguson adopt this
emendation, while recognizing that 'lowliest' (meaning 'humblest') is plausible.

10

The cruel Herod was not moved to ruth –
Then why grieves Mariam Herod's death to hear?
Why joy I not the tongue no more shall speak
That yielded forth my brother's latest doom?   40
Both youth and beauty might thy fury break
And both in him did ill befit a tomb.
And, worthy grandsire, ill did he requite
His high ascent, alone by thee procured,
Except he murdered thee to free the sprite   45
Which still he thought on earth too long immured.
How happy was it that Sohemus' mind
Was moved to pity my distressed estate!
Might Herod's life a trusty servant find,
My death to his had been unseparate.   50
These thoughts have power his death to make me bear:
Nay, more, to wish the news may firmly hold.
Yet cannot this repulse some falling tear
That will against my will some grief unfold.
And more I owe him for his love to me –   55
The deepest love that ever yet was seen –
Yet had I rather much a milkmaid be
Than be the monarch of Judea's queen.
It was for nought but love he wished his end
Might, to my death, but the vaunt-courier prove,   60
But I had rather still be foe than friend

37   *ruth* compassion (*OED*, *ruth*, 1).
40   *latest* recent.
41   i.e. Herod's fury might have been abated by Aristobolus's youth and beauty.
43   *requite* repay.
44   *ascent* ed. (Assent Q).
45   *Except* Unless.
      sprite Aristobolus's spirit.
46   *immured* imprisoned.
47   *mind* ed. (maide Q). The rhyme with 'find' (l. 49), as well as the sense of the line, argues for emendation.
49–50 If Herod had found a more reliable servant (than Sohemus), I would have been killed on Herod's death.
57–8   *Yet . . . queen* Weller and Ferguson compare this with *Antony and Cleopatra*, IV.xvi.75–7, and with Queen Elizabeth I's 1576 speech to parliament: 'If I were a milkmaid with a pail on my arm, whereby my person might be little set by, I would not forsake that poor state to match with the greatest monarch'.
60   *vaunt-courier* advance guard, forerunner. Compare *Lear*, III.ii.5.

11

To him that saves for hate, and kills for love.
Hard-hearted Mariam, at thy discontent
What floods of tears have drenched his manly face?
How canst thou, then, so faintly now lament   65
Thy truest lover's death, a death's disgrace?
Ay, now, mine eyes, you do begin to right
The wrongs of your admirer and my lord.
Long since you should have put your smiles to flight:
Ill doth a widowed eye with joy accord.   70
Why, now, methinks, the love I bare him then,
When virgin freedom left me unrestrained,
Doth to my heart begin to creep again.
My passion now is far from being feigned.
But, tears, fly back and hide you in your banks: 75
You must not be to Alexandra seen,
For if my moan be spied, but little thanks
Shall Mariam have from that incensèd queen.

ACT I, SCENE ii

[*Enter to*] MARIAM, ALEXANDRA

ALEXANDRA
What means these tears? My Mariam doth mistake:
The news we heard did tell the tyrant's end.
What, weep'st thou for thy brother's murder's sake?

---

62   *saves . . . love* Oxymoronic. Compare *Othello*, V.ii.45: 'That death's unnatural that kills for loving'.
65–6   How can you disgrace your true lover's death by lamenting it so faintly?
67–8   *now . . . lord* Apostrophising her own eyes, Mariam admits she is finally beginning to cry, thus correcting the wrong she has done to Herod (her eyes' 'admirer') by not weeping over his death.
74   *passion* emotion.
75   *hide . . . banks* Purkiss links this moment to the images of Niobe and Phaeton's sisters in the Countess of Pembroke's closet drama, *Antonius*.
78   *incensèd* enraged.

0   s.d. ed. (Actus primus: Scoena Secunda Q).
3   *murder's* ed. (murthers Q). Weller and Ferguson emend to 'murd'rer's', although 'murder's' makes sense. Alexandra asks whether Mariam is still weeping over Aristobolus's murder, because nobody, she believes, could lament for Herod.

12

Will ever wight a tear for Herod spend?
My curse pursue his breathless trunk and spirit,　　　　　5
Base Edomite, the damnèd Esau's heir.
Must he, ere Jacob's child, the crown inherit?
Must he, vile wretch, be set in David's chair?
No: David's soul, within the bosom placed
Of our forefather Abram, was ashamed　　　　　　　　10
To see his seat with such a toad disgraced,
That seat that hath by Judah's race been fained.
Thou fatal enemy to royal blood,
Did not the murder of my boy suffice
To stop thy cruel mouth that gaping stood,　　　　　　15
But must thou dim the mild Hircanus' eyes,
My gracious father, whose too ready hand
Did lift this Idumean from the dust?
And he, ungrateful caitiff, did withstand
The man that did in him most friendly trust.　　　　　20
What kingdom's right could cruel Herod claim?
Was he not Esau's issue, heir of hell?
Then what succession can he have but shame?
Did not his ancestor his birthright sell?

4　*wight* person.
6　The Edomites were the descendants of Esau (Genesis 36), who was the son of Isaac and older twin brother of Jacob, father of the Israelites. Esau sold Jacob his birthright for a pot of lentil pottage (Genesis 25, 29–34).
7　*ere* before.
　　Jacob's child presumably Aristobolus, Alexandra's son, who could claim descent from Jacob only by virtue of his Jewish faith, and not through blood (see I.ii.67n. below).
8　*David's chair* David's throne (with the sense also of his royal authority over the Jews).
9–10　*bosom . . . Abram* The place where the righteous dead await Judgement Day (see Luke 16.22–6). Abraham was the patriarch of God's chosen people: see Genesis 11–25.
12　*Judah's race* ed. (*Iudas* race Q). Judah was the son of Jacob and Leah and the founder of the tribe of Israelites. Abraham (ll. 9–10n. above) was his great-grandfather.
　　fained made glad (*OED, fain, v¹ b²*).
18　*Idumean* Herod. See note to 'Antipater' in 'Argument' above.
19　*caitiff* wretch, miserable person.
　　withstand oppose.
22　*Esau's issue* The Idumeans were descended from Esau. See note to 'Antipater' in 'Argument' above.
24　*birthright* See 6n. above and Genesis 25.29–34.

Oh, yes, he doth from Edom's name derive   25
His cruel nature which with blood is fed
That made him me of sire and son deprive:
He ever thirsts for blood, and blood is red.
Weep'st thou because his love to thee was bent,
And read'st thou love in crimson characters?   30
Slew he thy friends to work thy heart's content?
No: hate may justly call that action hers.
He gave the sacred priesthood, for thy sake,
To Aristobolus, yet doomed him dead
Before his back the Ephod warm could make,   35
And ere the mitre settled on his head.
Oh, had he given my boy no less than right,
The double oil should to his forehead bring
A double honour, shining doubly bright:
His birth anointed him both priest and king.   40
And say my father and my son he slew
To royalise by right your prince-born breath,
Was love the cause, can Mariam deem it true
That Herod gave commandment for her death?
I know, by fits, he showed some signs of love –   45
And yet not love, but raging lunacy –
And this his hate to thee may justly prove
That sure he hates Hircanus' family.
Who knows if he – inconstant, wavering lord –
His love to Doris had renewed again,   50
And, that he might his bed to her afford,
Perchance he wished that Mariam might be slain?

---

25   *Edom* The name given to Esau in the Hebrew bible.
26, 28, 30 *blood, red, crimson* Esau is supposed to have been born red and hairy (Genesis
        25.25). Here, this is seen to ally him with blood and bloodthirstiness.
29   *bent* directed, inclined.
34   *doomed* sentenced, destined.
35   *Ephod* ceremonial garment worn by the high priest (see Exodus 28.6–14; 39.1–26).
36   *mitre* headdress of a priest.
38   *double oil* Aristobolus's birthright should have seen him doubly anointed with oil
        as both high priest and king.
44   *Herod* ed. (*Mariam* Q) Dunstan and Greg first emended 'Mariam' to 'Herod' which
        fits the metre and sense. The repetition of 'Mariam' was probably a compositor's
        error.
49   *inconstant . . . lord* Alexandra transfers the traditionally feminine notion of
        inconstancy to Herod. Compare 'To Diana's Earthly Deputess,' l. 9; and IV.vi.67.

[MARIAM]

Doris! Alas, her time of love was past.
Those coals were raked in embers long ago,
If Mariam's love and she was now disgraced;   55
Nor did I glory in her overthrow.
He not a whit his first-born son esteemed
Because, as well as his, he was not mine.
My children only for his own he deemed;
These boys that did descend from royal line.   60
These did he style his heirs to David's throne:
My Alexander, if he live, shall sit   → son w/ Herod
In the majestic seat of Solomon.
To will it so did Herod think it fit.

ALEXANDRA

Why, who can claim from Alexander's brood   65
That gold-adornèd, lion-guarded chair?
Was Alexander not of David's blood
And was not Mariam Alexander's heir?
What more than right could Herod then bestow,
And who will think, except for more than right,   70
He did not raise them, for they were not low,
But born to wear the crown in his despite.

52   s.p. MARIAM ed. (*Nun:* Q).
53–5 *Alas . . . disgraced* A syntactically difficult passage which implies Herod's love for
       Doris is extinguished and could not be renewed *even* if Mariam and Mariam's love
       for Herod were disgraced.
55   Weller and Ferguson emend 'If' to 'Of', following Dunstan and Greg, while Purkiss
       notes the line makes sense as it stands. 'She' refers to Mariam, not Doris.
       disgraced ed. (disgrast Q). The original spelling ensures a more complete rhyme
       with 'past' (l. 53).
57   *first-born son* Antipater, Herod's son with Doris.
62   *Alexander* Mariam's son with Herod.
63   *seat of Solomon* Compare l. 8 and l. 61 above. Solomon inherited the throne of
       Israel from David, his father (1 Kings 2.1–12).
65   *Alexander's brood* Alexandra is referring to the descendants, not of her grandson,
       but of Alexander Jannaeus, her grandfather, and Alexander, her husband (and
       cousin), the son of Aristobolus II.
66   *lion-guarded* The lion was the symbol of the Israelite tribe of Judah, perhaps
       derived from Genesis 49.9 where Jacob calls his son Judah a 'lion's whelp'.
67   *Alexander . . . blood* Salome is incorrect here. Although Alexander Jannaeus
       presented himself as another King David, he was not lineally descended from him.
69–71 Alexandra's words undermine Herod's authority as she explains her children's
       heritage gave them every right to the throne, and Herod's actions only affirmed
       what was already theirs.
72   i.e. In spite of Herod, David's heirs were born to wear the crown.

15

Then send those tears away that are not sent
To thee by reason, but by passion's power.
Thine eyes to cheer, thy cheeks to smiles be bent,   75
And entertain with joy this happy hour.
Felicity, if when she comes she finds
A mourning habit and a cheerless look,
Will think she is not welcome to thy mind
And so perchance her lodging will not brook.   80
Oh, keep her whilst thou hast her. If she go,
She will not easily return again.
Full many a year have I endured in woe,
Yet still have sued her presence to obtain:
And did not I to her as presents send   85
A table, that best art did beautify,
Of two, to whom heaven did best feature lend,
To woo her love by winning Antony?
For when a prince's favour we do crave,
We first their <u>minions' loves</u> do seek to win.   90
So I, that sought Felicity to have,
Did with her <u>minion</u> Antony begin.
With double sleight I sought to captivate
The warlike lover, but I did not right,
For if my gift had borne but half the rate,   95
The Roman had been overtaken quite,
But now he farèd like a hungry guest
That to some plenteous festival is gone.
Now this, now that, he deems to eat were best:
Such choice doth make him let them all alone.   100
The boy's large forehead first did fairest seem;
Then glanced his eye upon my Mariam's cheek,
And that without comparison did deem:
What was in either but he most did leeke.

---

77   *Felicity* Happiness or good fortune, imagined here as a personification. See l. 92
     where Antony is described as fortune's 'minion'.
80   *brook* enjoy, make use of (*OED*, *brook*, *v.* 1).
86   *table* picture. Josephus explains how Alexandra sent 'pictures of her two children'
     to Antony to solicit his aid (*Ant.*, 15.2.384).
87   *two* Alexandra's two children, Aristobolus and Mariam.
90   *minions'* servants'. The term also carried connotations of sexual enslavement and
     might therefore emphasise Antony's lust for Cleopatra.
93   *double sleight* double cunning (because she sent pictures of both her children).
95   *rate* amount.

And thus distracted, either's beauty's might   105
Within the other's excellence was drowned.
Too much delight did bear him from delight,
For either's love, the other's did confound.
Where if thy portraiture had only gone,
His life from Herod, Antony had taken.   110
He would have lovèd thee, and thee alone,
And left the brown Egyptian clean forsaken.
And Cleopatra then to seek had been
So firm a lover of her wanèd face.
Then great Antonius' fall we had not seen   115
By her that fled to have him hold the chase.
Then Mariam in a Roman's chariot set
In place of Cleopatra might have shown
A mart of beauties in her visage met,
And part in this, that they were all her own.   120

104   *leeke* Dunstan and Greg suggest emending to 'seek', while Weller and Ferguson note
       the spelling 'may merely represent contemporary pronunciation of *like*'. The *OED*
       gives 'leeke' as a variant form of 'like'.
105   *might* strength, power.
107   Weller and Ferguson note this line is a version of the Ovidian topos, 'Inopem me
       copia fecit' ('Plenty has made me poor'), *Metamorphoses*, 3.466.
       bear ed. (bare Q). Weller and Ferguson note the 'semantic range of this word
       probably includes "bear" (carry away), "bare" (strip) and "bar" (deprive of or debar
       from); "bare" is a possible seventeenth-century spelling for all three meanings'.
108   *confound* bring to nothing.
109   *only gone* been sent on its own.
112   *Egyptian* Cleopatra. Mariam is presented throughout as a type of anti-Cleopatra:
       see Introduction.
113   *to seek had been* would have had to search for.
114   *wanèd face* A reference to Cleopatra's age and past beauties.
116   *fled . . . chase* Cleopatra fled from the naval battle of Actium, giving victory to
       Caesar because Antony followed her. See Shakespeare's *Antony and Cleopatra*, III.x,
       and the Countess of Pembroke's *Antonius* (1592), H1r–v.
117–18 The ostensible meaning is that Mariam might have taken Cleopatra's place in
       Antony's chariot. However, in Shakespeare's play, Cleopatra commits suicide to
       avoid being displayed in a Roman triumph (see *Antony and Cleopatra*, V.ii).
119   *mart* market. Mariam's beauties are presented by her mother as if for sale. Purkiss
       notes that Alexandra's words contrast with Mariam's virtuous response.
       visage face.
120   *And . . . this* 'And, part of this [was]', or 'And, an aspect of this [was]'. Dunstan and
       Greg emend to 'Apart' (i.e. singular and distinctive). Alexander Dyce, the Victorian
       editor and book collector, emended his personal quarto to read 'past' (i.e. sur-
       passed). The quarto is now in the Victoria and Albert Museum.
       all her own Mariam's beauties, unlike Cleopatra's, were not enhanced by cosmetics.

MARIAM

Not to be empress of aspiring Rome
Would Mariam like to Cleopatra live:
With purest body will I press my tomb,
And wish no favours Antony could give.

Cleopatra as this symbol of a "bad" woman

ALEXANDRA

Let us retire us that we may resolve   125
How now to deal in this reversèd state:
Great are th' affairs that we must now revolve,
And great affairs must not be taken late.

ACT I, SCENE iii

[*Enter to*] MARIAM [*and*] ALEXANDRA, SALOME

Herod's sister

SALOME

More plotting yet? Why, now you have the thing
For which so oft you spent your suppliant breath,
And Mariam hopes to have another king:
Her eyes do sparkle joy for Herod's death.

ALEXANDRA

If she desired another king to have,   5
She might, before she came in Herod's bed,
Have had her wish. More kings than one did crave
For leave to set a crown upon her head.

121–2   Mariam would not live like Cleopatra, even to be empress of Rome.
124   Compare with Marston's *Sophonisba* (1604–6): 'all that I crave / Is but chaste life or
        an untainted grave' (*Sophonisba*, III.i.129–30). Cleopatra was notorious for her
        affairs with Pompey, Caesar and Antony (see *Antony and Cleopatra*, III.xiii.
        117–21).
128   *late* Weller and Ferguson note there is a possible aural pun on 'light' (that is,
        lightly).

0   s.d. ed. (Actus primus. Scoena tertia. Q).
2   *suppliant breath* Salome suggests that Alexandra and Mariam have been praying for
        Herod's death.
3   *another king* Salome reveals her own character by implying that Mariam desires to
        remarry quickly.
8   *leave* permission.

I think with more than reason she laments
That she is freed from such a sad annoy: 10
Who is't will weep to part from discontent?
And, if she joy, she did not causeless joy.

SALOME

You durst not thus have given your tongue the rein,
If noble Herod still remained in life.
Your daughter's betters far, I dare maintain, 15
Might have rejoiced to be my brother's wife.

MARIAM

My betters far, base woman: 'tis untrue.
You scarce have ever my superiors seen,
For Mariam's servants were as good as you
Before she came to be Judea's queen. 20

SALOME

Now stirs the tongue that is so quickly moved,
But more than once your choler have I borne.
Your fumish words are sooner said than proved,
And Salome's reply is only scorn.

MARIAM

Scorn those that are for thy companions held. 25
Though I thy brother's face had never seen,
My birth thy baser birth so far excelled
I had to both of you the princess been.
Thou parti-Jew and parti-Edomite,

9   *more than reason* unreasonably.
10   *annoy* vexation, trouble.
11–12 i.e. Who will not weep to part from unhappiness? And if she is happy, she is not
       happy without reason.
13   Salome castigates Alexandra and Mariam for their outspokenness in a
       prefiguration of the accusations that lead to Mariam's death. See IV.vii.73–80.
17–18 *My . . . seen* Josephus notes that Salome's malice towards Mariam arose because 'in
       a certain debate, Mariam had in her rage despitefully hit [her] in the teeth with
       [her] obscure birth' (*Ant.*, 15.4.388).
21   See l. 13n. above.
22   *choler* ed. (collor Q). Anger, caused by an imbalance of yellow bile, one of the four
       humours thought to regulate the body's physical health. Purkiss notes Q's spelling
       also alludes to the colours of rhetoric: Salome has borne Mariam's angry speeches
       before.
23   *fumish* hot-tempered, alluding to the fumes of choler that disrupt the body's
       equilibrium.
29   *parti . . . Edomite* The Edomites were forced to convert to Judaism by John
       Hircanus and were therefore not regarded as full Jews.
       parti . . . parti part of one sort and part of another.

Thou mongrel, issued from rejected race,   30
Thy ancestors against the heavens did fight,
And thou, like them, wilt heavenly birth disgrace.

SALOME
Still twit you me with nothing but my birth?
What odds betwixt your ancestors and mine?
Both born of Adam, both were made of earth,   35
And both did come from holy Abraham's line.

MARIAM
I favour thee when nothing else I say.
With thy black acts, I'll not pollute my breath,
Else to thy charge I might full justly lay
A shameful life, besides a husband's death.   40

SALOME
'Tis true indeed, I did the plots reveal
That passed betwixt your favourites and you.
I meant not, I, a traitor to conceal.
Thus Salome your minion Joseph slew.

MARIAM
Heaven, dost thou mean this infamy to smother?   45
Let slandered Mariam ope thy closèd ear:
Self-guilt hath ever been suspicious mother,
And therefore I this speech with patience bear.
No, had not Salome's unsteadfast heart
In Josephus' stead her Constabarus placed,   50
To free herself, she had not used the art
To slander hapless Mariam for unchaste.

ALEXANDRA
Come, Mariam, let us go. It is no boot
To let the head contend against the foot.

[Exeunt MARIAM *and* ALEXANDRA]

---

30   *rejected race* because Esau gave away his birthright. See also the apocryphal 2
     Esdras 3.16: '[thou] didst choose Jacob, and cast off Esau'.
33   i.e. Do you still only taunt me with my birth?
34   *odds* difference.
44   *minion* servant (but compare I.ii.90n.): Salome implies that Joseph was sexually in
     thrall to Mariam.
47   i.e. Guiltiness has always bred suspicion. Weller and Ferguson emend to 'suspicion's
     mother', but the line makes sense as it stands.
52   *hapless* unlucky.

ACT I, SCENE iv

SALOME, *sola*

SALOME

Lives Salome to get so base a style
As foot to the proud Mariam? Herod's spirit
In happy time for her endured exile,
For did he live, she should not miss her merit.
But he is dead and, though he were my brother,   5
His death such store of cinders cannot cast
My coals of love to quench, for though they smother
The flames a while, yet will they out at last.
Oh, blest Arabia, in best climate placed,
I, by the fruit, will censure of the tree: 10
'Tis not in vain thy happy name thou hast,
If all Arabians like Silleus be.   *lover*
Had not my fate been too, too contrary
When I on Constabarus first did gaze,
Silleus had been object to mine eye,   15
Whose looks and personage must all eyes amaze.

53–4   *It . . . foot* Invoking the image of the body politic, Alexandra's words conclude the
        discourse on social rank that has structured this scene. Compare Elizabeth I's
        speech to parliament in 1566: 'I will deal therein for your safety and offer it unto
        you as your prince and head, without request. For it is monstrous that the feet
        should direct the head' (see Bell, 19).

0   s.d. ed. (Actus primus. Scoena quarta. Q).
        sola alone.
1   *so . . . style* so lowly a title.
2–3   *Herod's . . . exile* It is fortunate for Mariam that Herod has died.
4   *she . . . merit* she'd get what she deserves.
6–7   *store . . . quench* Compare the description of Herod's failed love for Doris at I.ii.54.
9   *blest Arabia* Weller and Ferguson note that Cary plays on the name 'Arabia Felix'
        'which Ptolemy and other ancient geographers gave to the fertile part of Arabia
        south of the Gulf of Aquaba'.
        placed ed. (plast Q). Q's spelling provides a more complete rhyme with 'last', l. 8.
10   i.e. I'll judge the tree by its fruit. See Matthew 7:17–20: 'A good tree cannot bring
        forth evil fruit . . . Therefore by their fruits ye shall know them'.
14–15   *gaze . . . eye* Salome appropriates the power of the gaze, making first Constabarus
        and then Silleus into desired objects.
16   *all eyes* ed. (allyes Q). The spelling in the printed text makes a visual pun between
        'all eyes' and 'allies'.

But now, ill-fated Salome, thy tongue
To Constabarus by itself is tied,
And now, except I do the Ebrew wrong,
I cannot be the fair Arabian bride.   20
What childish lets are these? Why stand I now
On honourable points? 'Tis long ago
Since shame was written on my tainted brow,
And certain 'tis that shame is honour's foe.
Had I upon my reputation stood,   25
Had I affected an unspotted life,
Josephus' veins had still been stuffed with blood,
And I to him had lived a sober wife.
Then had I never cast an eye of love
On Constabarus' now-detested face,   30
Then had I kept my thoughts without remove,
And blushed at motion of the least disgrace.
But shame is gone, and honour wiped away,
And Impudency on my forehead sits.
She bids me work my will without delay,   35
And for my will I will employ my wits.
He loves; I love: what then can be the cause
Keeps me from being the Arabian's wife?
It is the principles of Moses' laws,
For Constabarus still remains in life.   40
If he to me did bear as earnest hate
As I to him, for him there were an ease:

17–18   *tongue . . . tied* Salome's vows have tied her to Constabarus in marriage. The
        conjunction of 'tongue' and 'tied' at the end of the lines underscores this fate and
        also obliquely emphasises early modern injunctions about female silence and
        wifely obedience.
  19   *Ebrew* Constabarus.
  21   *lets* impediments.
  22   *points* arguments (*OED, point, n.* 1, 10 a).
  23   *tainted brow* Compare the description of Cleopatra's 'wanèd face' at I.ii.114. Sexual
        incontinency is seen to stain in both a moral and a physical manner. Weller and
        Ferguson point out there is also a probable reference to blushing here, as well as a
        suggestion of branding.
  28   *sober* dignified, sedate in demeanour (*OED, sober, a,* 5a).
  31   *without remove* without transferring or changing them.
  38   *from* ed. (for Q).
  39   *Moses' laws* the ten commandments, specifically, in this instance, 'thou shalt not
        commit adultery' (see Exodus 20.2–17 and Deuteronomy 5.6–21).

A separating bill might free his fate
From such a yoke that did so much displease.
Why should such privilege to man be given,
Or, given to them, why barred from women then?   45
Are men than we in greater grace with heaven,
Or cannot women hate as well as men?
I'll be the custom-breaker and begin
To show my sex the way to freedom's door,
And with an off'ring will I purge my sin: 50
The law was made for none but who are poor.
If Herod had lived, I might to him accuse
My present lord, but for the future's sake.
Then would I tell the king he did refuse   55
The sons of Baba in his power to take.
But now I must divorce him from my bed,
That my Silleus may possess his room.
Had I not begged his life, he had been dead.
I curse my tongue, the hinderer of his doom.   60
But then my wandering heart to him was fast,
Nor did I dream of change. Silleus said
He would be here and, see, he comes at last.
Had I not named him, longer had he stayed.

43   *separating bill* bill of divorce. Deuteronomy 24.1 makes issuing a 'bill of
      divorcement' a strictly masculine privilege. See Introduction for a discussion of
      contemporary ideas about divorce and divorce cases.
45–6 *Why . . . then?* The statement is a radical one for a female character. Cary places
      Salome in dialogue with Josephus, whose *Antiquity* reads: '[Salome] sent a libel of
      divorce to her husband, notwithstanding it were against the laws and ordinary
      customs of the Jews. For according to our ordinances, it is only lawful for the
      husband to do the same' (*Ant.*, 15.11.400).
47   For an analogous sentiment, penned by a woman, see Aemilia Lanyer, *Salve Deus
      Rex Judeaorum* (1611), D1r–v.
49   *custom-breaker* Early feminist readings took this as agreeably rebellious, but, if so,
      as Purkiss notes, Cary is equating proto-feminism with promiscuity, lying and
      murder.
51   *off'ring* Salome will lead her sex to 'freedom', changing social mores and thus
      eradicating the stigma attached to her actions.
52   Perhaps an oblique reference to the Penelope Rich divorce (see Introduction).
54   *but . . . sake* only for the sake of my future husband (i.e. Silleus).
56   *take* capture.
60   *curse my tongue* Compare ll. 17–18 above.
64   *Had . . . stayed* Salome suggests that speaking Silleus's name has called him to her.

ACT I, SCENE v

[*Enter to*] SALOME, SILLEUS

SILLEUS

    Well found, fair Salome, Judea's pride.
    Hath thy innated wisdom found the way
    To make Silleus deem him deified
    By gaining thee, a more-than-precious prey?

SALOME

    I have devised the best I can devise: 5
    A more imperfect means was never found.
    But what cares Salome? It doth suffice
    If our endeavours with their end be crowned.
    In this our land we have an ancient use,
    Permitted first by our law-giver's head: 10
    Who hates his wife, though for no just abuse,
    May with a bill divorce her from his bed.
    But in this custom women are not free:
    Yet I for once will wrest it. Blame not thou
    The ill I do, since what I do 's for thee: 15
    Though others blame, Silleus should allow.

SILLEUS

    Thinks Salome Silleus hath a tongue
    To censure her fair actions? Let my blood
    Bedash my proper brow, for such a wrong,
    The being yours, can make even vices good.   20
    Arabia, joy: prepare thy earth with green.
    Thou never happy wert indeed till now.
    Now shall thy ground be trod by beauty's queen:
    Her foot is destined to depress thy brow.
    Thou shalt, fair Salome, command as much   25

    0 s.d. (Actus primus. Soena quinta. Q).
    2 *innated* inborn.
    4 *prey* Salome is Silleus's prey. 'Prey' is used here in the positive sense of a 'prize' (see
       OED, prey, n. 3b: 'something saved or recovered from a contest or trial').
    9 *use* custom.
   10 *law-giver's* Moses's.
   11 *Who hates* He who hates.
   11 *no just abuse* no real reason.
   19 *proper* own.

As if the royal ornament were thine:
The weakness of Arabia's king is such
The kingdom is not his so much as mine.
My mouth is our Obodas' oracle,
Who thinks not aught but what Silleus will.   30
And thou, rare creature, Asia's miracle,
Shalt be to me as it: Obodas' still.

SALOME

'Tis not for glory I thy love accept:
Judea yields me honour's worthy store.
Had not affection in my bosom crept   35
My native country should my life deplore.
Were not Silleus he with whom I go,
I would not change my Palestine for Rome.
Much less would I, a glorious state to show,
Go far to purchase an Arabian tomb.   40

homeland loyalty

SILLEUS

Far be it from Silleus so to think.
I know it is thy gratitude requites
The love that is in me, and shall not shrink
Till death do sever me from earth's delights.

SALOME

But, whist: methinks the wolf is in our talk.   45
Be gone, Silleus. Who doth here arrive?
'Tis Constabarus that doth hither walk:
I'll find a quarrel, him from me to drive.   → *scuinto drivero?*

SILLEUS

Farewell, but were it not for thy command,
In his despite, Silleus here would stand.   [*Exit*]   50

---

26   *the royal ornament* the crown.
27   *Arabia's king* Obodas. Probably Obodas III.
30   i.e. Obodas only thinks what Silleus wishes him to.
32   *it* an oracle. Weller and Ferguson gloss these lines: 'Thou shalt be to me as an oracle, and that oracle, expressing our combined wills, shall still have power to govern Obodas'.
36   i.e. I would bewail the loss of my native country all my life.
37   *whom* ed. (home Q).
45   *whist* be silent.
     the wolf is in our talk Lat. *lupus in fabula*, meaning 'speak of the wolf', or, more commonly in English, 'speak of the devil'.
50   *In his despite* In spite of him, but also with a sense of 'in contempt of him'.

ACT I, SCENE vi

[*Enter to*] SALOME, CONSTABARUS

CONSTABARUS

Oh, Salome, how much you wrong your name,
Your race, your country, and your husband most!
A stranger's private conference is shame:
I blush for you, that have your blushing lost.
Oft have I found, and found you to my grief,   5
Consorted with this base Arabian here.
Heaven knows that you have been my comfort chief,
Then do not now my greater plague appear.
Now by the stately, carvèd edifice
That on Mount Sion makes so fair a show,   10
And by the altar fit for sacrifice,
I love thee more than thou thyself dost know.
Oft with a silent sorrow have I heard
How ill Judea's mouth doth censure thee,
And, did I not thine honour much regard,   15
Thou should'st not be exhorted thus for me.
Didst thou but know the worth of honest fame,
How much a virtuous woman is esteemed,
Thou would'st like hell eschew deservèd shame,
And seek to be both chaste and chastely deemed.   20
Our wisest prince did say, and true he said,
A virtuous woman crowns her husband's head.

---

0   s.d. ed. (Actus primus: Soena Sexta. Q).
3   i.e. For a woman to speak privately with a strange man is shameful.
4   Compare Salome's description of her 'tainted brow' at I.iv.23.
6   *Consorted with* In the company of, but also with undertones of 'having sexual
    commerce with' (*OED*, consort, *v*. I.1 and 2).
    base lowly.
9   *edifice* the Temple on the Mount, built by Solomon at the behest of King David and
    intended to house the Ark of the Covenant (see 1 Kings 6).
14 i.e. How badly you are criticised in Judea.
19 *eschew* avoid.
20 *chaste . . . deemed* This recalls the sentiment Cary inscribed on a ring for one of her
    daughters: 'Be and seem'.
21 *Our wisest prince* King Solomon (see Proverbs 12.4: 'A virtuous woman is the
    crown of her husband').

SALOME

    Did I for this uprear thy low estate?
    Did I for this requital beg thy life
    That thou had'st forfeited? Hapless fate,   25
    To be to such a thankless wretch the wife.
    This hand of mine hath lifted up thy head,
    Which many a day ago had fall'n full low
    Because the sons of Baba are not dead:
    To me thou dost both life and fortune owe.   30

CONSTABARUS

    You have my patience often exercised:
    Use, make my choler keep within the banks.
    Yet boast no more, but be by me advised:
    A benefit upbraided, forfeits thanks.
    I prithee, Salome, dismiss this mood: 35
    Thou dost not know how ill it fits thy place.
    My words were all intended for thy good,
    To raise thine honour and to stop disgrace.

SALOME

    To stop disgrace? Take thou no care for me!
    Nay, do thy worst: thy worst I set not by.   40
    No shame of mine is like to light on thee:
    Thy love and admonitions I defy.
    Thou shalt no hour longer call me wife.
    Thy jealousy procures my hate so deep
    That I from thee do mean to free my life   45
    By a divorcing bill before I sleep.

CONSTABARUS

    Are Hebrew women now transformed to men?
    Why do you not as well our battles fight,

---

25   *forfeited? Hapless* ed. (forfeited haples Q). The line is not iambic which suggests
     textual corruption. Most editors emend it to read: 'That thou had'st forfeited to
     hapless fate'. However, a change in punctuation restores sense, if not metre.

32   *Use, make* Some editors emend to 'use makes', but the line makes sense as an
     apostrophe to 'use' or 'habit'.
     choler See I.iii.22n. above.

34   i.e. If you use a favour you have done for someone as a means of reproaching them,
     you forfeit any thanks for it.

40   *I . . . by* I couldn't care less about.

And wear our armour? Suffer this, and then
Let all the world be topsy turvied quite: 50
Let fishes graze, beasts swim, and birds descend;
Let fire burn downwards whilst the earth aspires;
Let winter's heat and summer's cold offend;
Let thistles grow on vines, and grapes on briars.
Set us to spin or sew, or, at the best,   55
Make us wood-hewers, water-bearing wights.
For sacred service, let us take no rest:
Use us as Joshua did the Gibonites.

SALOME

Hold on your talk, till it be time to end.
For me, I am resolved it shall be so.   60
Though I be first that to this course do bend,
I shall not be the last, full well I know.

CONSTABARUS

Why, then, be witness heaven, the judge of sins;
Be witness spirits that eschew the dark;
Be witness angels; witness cherubins,   65
Whose semblance sits upon the holy ark;
Be witness earth; be witness Palestine;
Be witness David's city, if my heart
Did ever merit such an act of thine,
Or if the fault be mine that makes us part.   70
Since mildest Moses, friend unto the Lord,

49–54 *Suffer . . . briars* This description of a world turned upside down parodies the
language of Petrarchan paradox, illustrating the disruptive potential of
Constabarus's uncontrollable beloved.

50–4   *Let . . . Let* See I.i.16–18n.

51   *swim* ed. (swine Q).

52   *aspires* rises up (*OED, aspire, v.* 5).

55   *spin or sew* A reference to Hercules's enslavement to Omphale, often employed in
Cary's time as an example of a man's unnatural debasement to a woman (see Ovid,
Fasti, 2.305).

56   *water-bearing* ed. (Waters-bearing Q).
       wights people (compare I.ii.4n.).

58   *Joshua . . . Gibonites* See Joshua 9.21–7.

64   *eschew* See l. 19n. above.

65   *cherubins* the second order of angels (*OED, cherub*, 2b.). Cherubim decorated the
sanctuary in the Temple that held the Ark of the Covenant (see 1 Kings 6.23–9).

66   *the holy ark* the Ark of the Covenant (see l. 9n. above).

68   *David's city* Jerusalem.

71–3   *Since . . . sword* See Exodus 11.

Did work his wonders in the land of Ham,
And slew the first-born babes without a sword
(In sign whereof we eat the holy lamb),
Till now, that fourteen hundred years are past   75
Since first the law with us hath been in force,
You are the first, and will, I hope, be last,
That ever sought her husband to divorce.

SALOME
I mean not to be led by precedent:
My will shall be to me instead of law.   80

CONSTABARUS
I fear me much, you will too late repent
That you have ever lived so void of awe.
This is Silleus' love that makes you thus
Reverse all order: you must next be his,
But, if my thoughts aright the cause discuss,   85
In winning you, he gains no lasting bliss.
I was Silleus and not long ago
Josephus then was Constabarus now.
When you became my friend you proved his foe,
As now for him you break to me your vow.   90

SALOME
If once I loved you, greater is your debt,
For certain 'tis that you deserved it not,
And undeservèd love we soon forget,
And therefore that to me can be no blot.
But now fare ill, my once-belovèd lord,   95
Yet never more beloved than now abhorred.   [Exit]

CONSTABARUS
Yet Constabarus biddeth thee farewell:
Farewell, light creature. Heaven forgive thy sin.
My prophesying spirit doth foretell
Thy wavering thoughts do yet but new begin.   100

---

72   *the land of Ham* Egypt (see, for example, Psalm 78.51).
74   *holy lamb* Eaten during the festival of Passover.
76   *the law* Moses's law.
80   This sentiment shows Salome's dangerously unruly nature at the same time as it links
       her to an early modern debate about the nature of tyranny (see Introduction).
89   *friend* lover.
       his Josephus's.
90   *him* Silleus.
       vow ed. (vowd Q).

Yet I have better 'scaped than Joseph did,
But if our Herod's death had been delayed,
The valiant youths that I so long have hid
Had been by her, and I for them, betrayed.
Therefore in happy hour did Caesar give   105
The fatal blow to wanton Antony,
For had he lived, our Herod then should live,
But great Antonius' death made Herod die.
Had he enjoyed his breath, not I alone
Had been in danger of a deadly fall,   110
But Mariam had the way of peril gone,
Though by the tyrant most beloved of all:
The sweet-faced Mariam, as free from guilt
As heaven from spots. Yet, had her lord come back,
Her purest blood had been unjustly spilt,   115
And Salome it was would work her wrack.
Though all Judea yield her innocent,
She often hath been near to punishment.   [*Exit*]

[CHORUS]

CHORUS
Those minds that wholly dote upon delight,
Except they only joy in inward good,   120
Still hope at last to hop upon the right,
And so from sand they leap in loathsome mud:
    Fond wretches, seeking what they cannot find,
    For no content attends a wavering mind.

If wealth they do desire and wealth attain,   125
Then wondrous fain would they to honour leap.

101   *better . . . did* Josephus, Salome's first husband, was put to death.
103   *valiant youths* Baba's sons.
116   *wrack* destruction.
117   *yield* declare, report (*OED*, *yield*, *v.* 12a and b).
118   s.p. CHORUS 'A company of Jews' (see 'The names of the speakers' above). Bell
       suggests the Chorus remain constantly on stage because no entries or exits are
       included in the stage directions (Bell, 30). The Chorus's remarks tend to be
       conservative and moralising, and it is debatable whether they should be regarded
       as reliable interpreters of the play's action.
120   *Except* Unless.
123   *Fond* Foolish.
126   *wondrous fain* joyously.
       leap ed. (lep Q). Q's spelling reinforces the rhyme with 'step' at l. 128 below.

Of mean degree, they do in honour gain:
They would but wish a little higher step.
   Thus step to step and wealth to wealth they add,
    Yet cannot all their plenty make them glad.   130

Yet oft we see that some in humble state
Are cheerful, pleasant, happy, and content,
When those, indeed, that are of higher state,
With vain additions do their thoughts torment.
   Th' one would to his mind his fortune bind;   135
   Th' other to his fortune frames his mind.

To wish variety is sign of grief,
For if you like your state as now it is,
Why should an alteration bring relief?
Nay, change would then be feared as loss of bliss.   140
   That man is only happy in his fate
   That is delighted in a settled state.

Still Mariam wished she from her lord were free,
For expectation of variety.
Yet now she sees her wishes prosperous be,   145
She grieves, because her lord so soon did die.
   Who can those vast imaginations feed,
   Where in a property contempt doth breed?

Were Herod now perchance to live again,
She would again as much be grieved at that.   150
All that she may, she ever doth disdain:
Her wishes guide her to she knows not what.
   And sad must be their looks, their honour sour,
   That care for nothing being in their power.

127   *Of* Weller and Ferguson, following Dunstan and Greg, emend to 'If'. However, the
     line makes sense as it stands: Lowly people who gain wealth (and, through wealth,
     honour), desire more and more wealth.
128   *step* Weller and Ferguson note that this plays on the buried etymology, and French
     meaning, of 'degree' (l. 127) as 'step'.
132   *cheerful* ed. (chreefull Q).
134   *vain* worthless.
148   i.e. Where what is possessed is despised (Carroll, ed.).
154   *being* that is.

ACT II, SCENE i

[Enter] PHERORAS *and* GRAPHINA

PHERORAS

    'Tis true, Graphina, now the time draws nigh
    Wherein the holy priest with hallowed right
    The happy, long-desirèd knot shall tie,
    Pheroras and Graphina to unite.
    How oft have I with lifted hands implored   5
    This blessed hour, till now implored in vain,
    Which hath my wishèd liberty restored
    And made my subject self my own again?
    Thy love, fair maid, upon mine eye doth sit,
    Whose nature hot doth dry the moisture all,   10
    Which were in nature and in reason fit
    For my monarchal brother's death to fall.
    Had Herod lived, he would have plucked my hand
    From fair Graphina's palm perforce, and tied
    The same in hateful and despisèd band,   15
    For I had had a baby to my bride.
    Scarce can her infant tongue with easy voice
    Her name distinguish to another's ear,

  0   s.d. ed. (*Actus secundus. Scoena prima.* Q).
  1   *Graphina* The name is Cary's invention (see '*The Names of the Speakers*' above).
  2   *right* also with the sense of 'rite'.
  3   *knot* of marriage.
  5   *How oft have I* Compare I.i.1. This verbal construction links Mariam and Pheroras who both suffer conflicted emotions about Herod's death.
  8   *my subject self* Pheroras was King Herod's subject and therefore owed obedience to him. Subjection, in this play, is complicated and not just experienced by its female characters.
9–10   *love . . . hot* In humoral theory, love was linked to the blood and to a hot, sanguine temperament that, here, dries Pheroras's tears. Compare I.iii.22n. above.
10–12   *dry . . . fall* Pheroras cannot weep for Herod's supposed death. Compare Mariam's opening lament, especially I.i.65–6.
 14   *perforce* forcibly, inevitably.
 16   *baby* Herod wished to marry Cypros, his daughter, to Pheroras (See *Ant.*, 16.11.424). Josephus does not, though, identify her as a baby: Richardson estimates she was between fourteen and sixteen years old (Richardson, *Herod*, 47, 275n.51).
17–20   *Scarce . . . swear* Herod's daughter (who can barely speak) and Herod's brother (who is enforced to speak against his desires) are similarly subordinate to Herod's will.

Yet had he lived, his power and not my choice
Had made me solemnly the contract swear.   20
Have I not cause in such a change to joy?
What though she be my niece, a princess born?
Near blood's without respect, high birth a toy,
Since love can teach blood and kindred's scorn.
What booted it that he did raise my head   25
To be his realm's co-partner, kingdom's mate?
Withal, he kept Graphina from my bed –
More wished by me than thrice Judea's state.
Oh, could not he be skilful judge in love,
That doted so upon his Mariam's face?   30
He for his passion Doris did remove;
I needed not a lawful wife displace.
It could not be but he had power to judge,
But he, that never grudged a kingdom's share,
This well-known happiness to me did grudge,   35
And meant to be therein without compare;
Else had I been his equal in love's host,
For though the diadem on Mariam's head
Corrupt the vulgar judgements, I will boast
Graphina's brow's as white, her cheeks as red.   40

22 *What though* What does it matter that.
24 Since love can teach one to scorn one's relatives. The line's imperfect scansion
    might set it apart as an apothegm, or indicate textual corruption.
25 *What booted it* What did it matter. (There is an echo here of I.iii.53–4.)
26 *co-partner . . . mate* The language here presents political alliance with Herod as a
    marriage. Here again, Pheroras's relationship to Herod is similar to that of
    Mariam.
27 *Withal* At the same time.
29, 33, 39 *judge, judge, judgements* As borne out by its Chorus, Act 2 is concerned with the
    notion of judgement, first articulated here. (For other references to judgement see
    I.i.6; I.vi.63; II.iv,117–46; IV.iii.64.)
32 *lawful* sanctioned by law.
33 i.e. He must have had the power to judge.
37 *his equal* In this interesting revision of social hierarchies, love, rather than political
    influence, grants equality. Compare II.i.8 above, where Pheroras speaks of his
    'subject self'.
39 *the vulgar judgements* the judgements of ordinary people. Pheroras indicates that
    Mariam's position places her in the public eye and subjects her to popular opinion.
40 *Graphina's* ed. (*Graphina* Q).
    white . . . red Pheroras invokes the language of love poetry, perhaps implicitly
    inviting Graphina to join him in composing a sonnet (Bell, 22).

Why speaks thou not, fair creature? Move thy tongue,
For silence is a sign of discontent.
It were to both our loves too great a wrong
If now this hour do find thee sadly bent.

GRAPHINA

Mistake me not, my lord. Too oft have I   45
Desired this time to come with wingèd feet
To be enwrapped with grief when 'tis too nigh –
You know my wishes ever yours did meet.
If I be silent, 'tis no more but fear
That I should say too little when I speak,   50
But since you will my imperfections bear,
In spite of doubt, I will my silence break.
Yet might amazement tie my moving tongue,
But that I know before Pheroras' mind.
I have admired your affection long   55
And cannot yet therein a reason find.
Your hand hath lifted me from lowest state
To highest eminency, wondrous grace,
And me, your handmaid, have you made your mate,
⌈Though all but you alone do count me base.⌋   60
You have preserved me pure at my request,
Though you so weak a vassal might constrain
To yield to your high will. Then, last not best,
In my respect, a princess you disdain.
Then need not all these favours study crave   65
To be requited by a simple maid?

41–2   Compare II.i.17–20 and note. It is important to Pheroras that his future wife can
       express her desires.
44   *sadly bent* inclined to sadness.
45   *Too oft have I* Compare II.i.5n. above. Graphina shares in Pheroras and Mariam's
       emotions about Herod's death.
47   *enwrapped* enveloped, but with a pun on 'rapt', i.e. 'in a trance'.
49   *but* than.
51   *my imperfections* Compare Mariam's apologies for the weakness of her gender:
       I.i.6–8.
54   i.e. Except I already know what Pheroras thinks.
56   *a reason find* for his love towards her.
61   *pure* virginal.
62   *vassal* servant, with a pun on 'weaker vessel'. See 1 Peter 3.7: 'Likewise, ye husbands
       [give] honour unto the woman, as unto the weaker vessel'.
64   *In my respect* Because of me.
65–6   i.e. Doesn't a simple maid need to study how to repay all the favours bestowed on her?

And study still, you know, must silence have;
Then be my cause for silence justly weighed.
But study cannot boot nor I requite,
Except your lowly handmaid's steadfast love   70
And fast obedience may your mind delight.
I will not promise more than I can prove.

PHERORAS

That study needs not let Graphina smile,
And I desire no greater recompense.
I cannot vaunt me in a glorious style,   75
Nor show my love in far-fetched eloquence,
But, this, believe me: never Herod's heart
Hath held his prince-born, beauty-famèd wife
In nearer place than thou, fair virgin, art
To him that holds the glory of his life.   80
Should Herod's body leave the sepulchre
And entertain the severed ghost again,
He should not be my nuptial hinderer
Except he hindered it with dying pain.
Come, fair Graphina, let us go in state   85
This wish-endearèd time to celebrate.

[*Exeunt*]

68   Graphina asks Pheroras to exercise his judgement on her silence prudently. Com-
     pare the Chorus's words at 125–6 below which condemn hasty conclusions.
69   *boot* be good or profitable.
     requite repay (Pheroras's favours).
71   *fast* firm.
72   *prove* demonstrate.
73–86 Pheroras's concluding lines form a sonnet.
73   i.e. Studying (how to repay Pheroras's favours) need not prevent Graphina from
     smiling.
75   *vaunt me* boast.
84   i.e. Unless he prevented it by killing me.

ACT II, SCENE ii

[*Enter*] CONSTABARUS *and* BABA'S SONS

FIRST SON

Now, valiant friend, you have our lives redeemed,
Which lives, as saved by you, to you are due.
Command and you shall see yourself esteemed:
Our lives and liberties belong to you.
This twice six years with hazard of your life   5
You have concealed us from the tyrant's sword –
Though cruel Herod's sister were your wife,
You durst, in scorn of fear, this grace afford.
In recompense, we know not what to say –
A poor reward were thanks for such a merit.   10
Our truest friendship at your feet we lay,
The best requital to a noble spirit.

CONSTABARUS

Oh, how you wrong our friendship, valiant youth.
With friends there is not such a word as debt;
Where amity is tied with bond of truth   15
All benefits are there in common set.
Then is the golden age with them renewed,
All names of properties are banished quite,
Division and distinction are eschewed,
Each hath to what belongs to others' right.   20
And 'tis not sure so full a benefit
Freely to give as freely to require.

---

  0   s.d. ed. (Actus 2. Soena. 2. Q).
  5   *twice six years* Josephus states that Baba's sons were hidden by Constabarus for
      twelve years (*Ant.*, 15.11.400).
  6   *the tyrant's* Herod's.
  7   *Herod's sister* Salome.
  8   i.e. In spite of fear, you dared accord us this grace (of hiding us).
 10   i.e. Thanks would be a poor reward for such a favour.
14–22 Cary's evocation of friendship and communal property reads like a rhetorical
      exercise on *Amicorum communia omnia*, the first of Erasmus's *Adages*. Purkiss
      suggests Cary might have incorporated a schoolroom exercise into her play.
 17   *golden age* mythical time of peace and prosperity, such as that experienced by
      Adam and Eve in the garden of Eden.
 20   i.e. Each has a right to what belongs to the others.

A bounteous act hath glory following it:
They cause the glory that the act desire.
All friendship should the pattern imitate   25
Of Jesse's son and valiant Jonathan,
For neither sovereign's nor father's hate
A friendship fixed on virtue sever can.
Too much of this: 'tis written in the heart,
And needs no amplifying with the tongue;   30
Now may you from your living tomb depart,
Where Herod's life hath kept you over long.
Too great an injury to a noble mind
To be quick buried. You had purchased fame
Some years ago, but that you were confined   35
While thousand meaner did advance their name.
Your best of life, the prime of all your years,
Your time of action is from you bereft.
Twelve winters have you over-passed in fears,
Yet if you use it well enough is left –   40
And who can doubt but you will use it well?
The sons of Baba have it by descent
In all their thoughts each action to excel,
Boldly to act and wisely to invent.

SECOND SON

Had it not like the hateful cuckoo been,   45
Whose riper age his infant nurse doth kill,
So long we had not kept ourselves unseen,
But Constabarus safely crossed our will.
For had the tyrant fixed his cruel eye

---

26   *Jesse's son* David (see 1 Samuel 17.12–2 Samuel 1.27). The friendship of David and
      Jonathan was proverbially faithful.
30   *needs* ed. (need Q).
34   *quick buried* buried alive.
36   *advance their name* become more famous.
44   *invent* plot (*OED, invent v.* 2.a).
45   *cuckoo* Cuckoos are renowned for laying their eggs in other birds' nests. After hatch-
      ing, the young cuckoo evicts all the other chicks and, in the early modern period,
      also had the reputation of killing the parent bird who fed it (see, for example,
      Gabriel Harvey, *The Trimming of Thomas Nashe*, 1597, B1v). Hiscock links the
      cuckoo image to Cary's interest 'in diverse forms of dispossession' (Andrew Hiscock,
      'The hateful cuckoo: Elizabeth Cary's *Tragedie of Mariam*, a Renaissance drama of
      dispossession', *Forum for Modern Language Studies* 33.2, 1997, 97–114, 97).
49   *the tyrant* Herod.

On our concealèd faces, wrath had swayed   50
His justice so that he had forced us die.
And dearer price than life we should have paid,
For you, our truest friend, had fallen with us,
And we, much like a house on pillars set,
Had clean depressed our prop, and therefore thus   55
Our ready will with our concealment met.
But now that you, fair lord, are dangerless,
The sons of Baba shall their rigour show,
And prove it was not baseness did oppress
Our hearts so long, but honour kept them low.   60

FIRST SON
Yet do I fear this tale of Herod's death
At last will prove a very tale indeed.
It gives me strongly in my mind, his breath
Will be preserved to make a number bleed.
I wish not therefore to be set at large,   65
Yet peril to myself I do not leer:
Let us for some days longer be your charge,
Till we of Herod's state the truth do hear.

CONSTABARUS
What! Art thou turned a coward, noble youth,
That thou begin'st to doubt undoubted truth?   70

FIRST SON
Were it my brother's tongue that cast this doubt,
I from his heart would have the question out
With this keen falchion, but 'tis you, my lord,
Against whose head I must not lift a sword,
I am so tied in gratitude.

50–1   *wrath . . . justice* This links to Act 2's theme of sensually corrupted judgement. See Chorus below and note to II.i.29, 33, 39n. above.

54–5   *house . . . prop* Possibly an oblique reference to Samson's destruction of the Philistines' house in Judges 16.25–31. By challenging Herod, Baba's sons would have destroyed their chief support (Constabarus) as well as themselves.

56   i.e. We consented to our concealment.

57   *dangerless* out of danger. Bell notes that this line begins a sonnet that ends with Constabarus's couplet at ll. 69–70.

62   *a very tale* very much a tale.

63–4   i.e. I have a strong premonition that [Herod] is still alive and will avenge himself.

66   *leer* look at askance. Weller and Ferguson emend to 'fear', but the line makes sense as it stands.

73   *falchion* sword, originally a broad sword.

CONSTABARUS   Believe   75
    You have no cause to take it ill.
    If any word of mine your heart did grieve,
    The word dissented from the speaker's will.
    I know it was not fear the doubt begun,
    But rather valour and your care of me –   80
    A coward could not be your father's son,
    Yet know I doubts unnecessary be,
    For who can think that in Antonius' fall,
    Herod, his bosom friend, should 'scape unbruised?
    Then, Caesar, we might thee an idiot call   85
    If thou by him should'st be so far abused.

SECOND SON
    Lord Constabarus, let me tell you this:
    Upon submission, Caesar will forgive,
    And therefore, though the tyrant did amiss,
    It may fall out that he will let him live.
    Not many years ago it is since I,   90
    Directed thither by my father's care,
    In famous Rome for twice twelve months did live,
    My life from Hebrews' cruelty to spare.
    There, though I were but yet of boyish age,   95
    I bent mine eye to mark, mine ears to hear,
    Where I did see Octavius, then a page,
    When first he did to Julian's sight appear.
    Methought I saw such mildness in his face,
    And such a sweetness in his looks did grow,   100
    Withal commixed with so majestic grace,
    His phys'nomy his fortune did foreshow.
    For this I am indebted to mine eye,
    But then mine ear received more evidence:
    By that I knew his love to clemency,   105

79   *begun* began.
88   *submission* a demonstration of submissiveness, but also with a sense of submitting
       to Caesar's judgement for a decision.
89   *the tyrant* Herod.
90   *he* Caesar.
97   *Octavius* Later, Octavius (or Augustus) Caesar. He was the adopted son of Julius Caesar.
98   *Julian's* Julius Caesar's.
102   *phys'nomy* facial features.

How he with hottest choler could dispense.

CONSTABARUS

But we have more than barely heard the news;
It hath been twice confirmed, and though some tongue
Might be so false with false report t' abuse,
A false report hath never lasted long.   110
But be it so that Herod have his life,
Concealment would not then a whit avail,
For certain 'tis that she that was my wife
Would not to set her accusation fail.
And therefore now as good the venture give   115
And free ourselves from blot of cowardice,
As show a pitiful desire to live,
For who can pity but they must despise?

FIRST SON

I yield, but to necessity I yield.
I dare upon this doubt engage mine arm: 120
That Herod shall again this kingdom wield
And prove his death to be a false alarm.

SECOND SON

I doubt it, too. God grant it be an error.
'Tis best without a cause to be in terror,
And rather had I, though my soul be mine,   125
My soul should lie than prove a true divine.

CONSTABARUS

Come, come! Let fear go seek a dastard's nest –
Undaunted courage lies in a noble breast.

                                                    [*Exeunt*]

---

106   *choler* Compare I.iii.22: Octavius can master his anger in a way that Salome
       believes Mariam cannot.
109–10 *false . . . long* Ironic, given Salome's false accusations of Mariam which lead to the
       latter's death.
126   *divine* prophet.
127   *dastard's* coward's.

ACT II, SCENE iii

[*Enter*] DORIS *and* ANTIPATER

sun

DORIS

You royal buildings, bow your lofty side
And scope to her that is by right your queen,
Let your humility upbraid the pride
Of those in whom no due respect is seen.
Nine times have we with trumpets' haughty sound,   5
And banishing sour leaven from our taste,
Observed the feast that takes the fruit from ground,
Since I, fair city, did behold thee last.
So long it is since Mariam's purer cheek   bitterness
Did rob from mine the glory, and so long   10
Since I returned my native town to seek —
And with me nothing but the sense of wrong,
And thee, my boy, whose birth, though great it were,
Yet have thy after-fortunes proved but poor.
When thou wert born, how little did I fear   15
Thou should'st be thrust from forth thy father's door.
Art thou not Herod's right-begotten son?
Was not the hapless Doris, Herod's wife?
Yes, ere he had the Hebrew kingdom won,

---

0   s.d. ed. (Actus 2. Scoena 3. Q).

1   *You* ed. (Your Q).

2   *scope* height. Purkiss reads 'scope' as a noun, interpreting the lines as: 'bow your
    walls and your height to Doris'. Weller and Ferguson emend to 'stoop'.

5   *trumpets' . . . sound* Silver trumpets called the congregation to a festival: see
    Numbers 10.8–10. Doris says she has not been to Jerusalem for nine years,
    although, historically, thirteen years had passed between her divorce and the events
    of the play.

6   *banishing . . . taste* The feast of unleavened bread took place on the day after
    Passover. See Exodus 13.6–7 and Leviticus 23.6.

7   *feast . . . ground* The feast of first fruits occurred soon after Passover. See Leviticus
    23.10–21.

11 *my native town* Jerusalem. In *Ant.*, Josephus says Doris was of Herod's 'own nation',
    while, in *Wars*, he states she was born in Jerusalem (*Wars*, 1.17.589).

15 *born* Antipater was born *c.* 46 BCE.

19, 22 *ere* before.

19–20 *Hebrew . . . life* Doris married Herod *c.* 47 BCE. He succeeded to the throne of Judea
    in 37 BCE, around the same time as he married Mariam.

41

I was companion to his private life.   20
Was I not fair enough to be a queen?
Why, ere thou wert to me, false monarch, tied,
My lake of beauty might as well be seen
As after I had lived five years thy bride.
Yet then thine oath came pouring like the rain,   25
Which all affirmed my face without compare,
And that, if thou might'st Doris' love obtain,
For all the world besides thou did'st not care.
Then was I young, and rich, and nobly born,
And therefore worthy to be Herod's mate,   30
Yet thou, ungrateful, cast me off with scorn
When heaven's purpose raised your meaner fate.
Oft have I begged for vengeance for this fact
And with dejected knees, aspiring hands,
Have prayed the highest power to enact   35
The fall of her that on my trophy stands.
Revenge I have according to my will,
Yet where I wished, this vengeance did not light –
I wished it should high-hearted Mariam kill,
But it against my whilom lord did fight.   40
With thee, sweet boy, I came, and came to try
If thou before his bastards might be placed
In Herod's royal seat and dignity,
But Mariam's infants here are only graced,
And now for us there doth no hope remain.   45
Yet we will not return till Herod's end
Be more confirmed: perchance he is not slain.
So glorious fortunes may my boy attend,
For if he live, he'll think it doth suffice
That he to Doris shows such cruelty –   50

[margin: fury of mother's bitterness to son]

[margin: actress Herod]

33   *Oft have I* Compare I.i.1, II.i.5 and 45.
34   *dejected ... aspiring* bent down, upraised.
39   *high-hearted Mariam* Like Salome, Doris accuses Mariam of pride (compare I.iii.33–4).
40   *whilom* former.
41   *sweet boy* Doris addresses Antipater.
42   *his bastards* Herod's children with Mariam.
46–7 Doris shares Baba's first son's doubts that Herod is not dead (compare II.ii.61–4).
49   *he* Herod.

For as he did my wretched life despise,
So do I know I shall despisèd die.
Let him but prove as natural to thee
As cruel to thy miserable mother,
His cruelty shall not upbraided be   55
But in thy fortunes. I his faults will smother.

ANTIPATER

Each mouth within the city loudly cries
That Herod's death is certain. Therefore, we   *meta*
Had best some subtle, hidden plot devise
That Mariam's children might subverted be   60
By poison's drink, or else by murderous knife.
So we may be advanced, it skills not how –
They are but bastards; you were Herod's wife,
And foul adultery blotteth Mariam's brow.

DORIS

They are too strong to be by us removed,   65
Or else revenge's foulest spotted face
By our detested wrongs might be approved,
But weakness must to greater power give place.
But let us now retire to grieve alone,
For solitariness best fitteth moan.   70

[*Exeunt*]

51–2   *wretched . . . die* Compare II.ii.115–18. The gender difference is clear: Doris accepts a pitied and despised condition while Constabarus and Baba's sons cannot contemplate it.

55   *upbraided* censured.

59   *subtle, hidden plot* Compare II.ii.44n. and Salome's machinations. The play takes place in an atmosphere of deceit and suspicion.

60   *subverted* overthrown, ruined.

62   *skills* matters.

64   *blotteth . . . brow* Compare with Salome's understanding of her own 'tainted brow' at I.iv.23.

70   Proverbial: see Tilley, S606.

ACT II, SCENE iv

[*Enter*] SILLEUS *and* CONSTABARUS

SILLEUS

    Well met, Judean lord, the only wight
    Silleus wished to see. I am to call
    Thy tongue to strict account.

CONSTABARUS   For what despite?

    I ready am to hear and answer all,
    But if directly at the cause I guess   5
    That breeds this challenge, you must pardon me
    And now some other ground of fight profess,
    For I have vowed. Vows must unbroken be.

SILLEUS

    What may be your expectation? Let me know.

CONSTABARUS

    Why, aught concerning Salome! My sword   10
    Shall not be wielded for a cause so low;
    A blow for her, my arm will scorn t' afford.

SILLEUS

    It is for slandering her unspotted name,
    And I will make thee, in thy vow's despite,
    Suck up the breath that did my mistress blame,   15
    And swallow it again to do her right.

CONSTABARUS

    I prithee, give some other quarrel ground.
    To find beginning, rail against my name,
    Or strike me first, or let some scarlet wound
    Inflame my courage; give me words of shame,   20

    0   s.d. ed. (Actus secundus. Scoena 4. Q).
    1   *wight* person.
  3, 22   *despite* contempt, malice.
    7   *ground of fight* reason for fighting.
    9   *expectation* Weller and Ferguson emend to 'exception' to repair the metre, but the
        line makes sense as it stands.
   10   *Salome* ed. (*Salom* Q).
   11   *wielded* ed. (welded Q).
   14   *in . . . despite* in spite of your vow.
   18   *rail . . . name* slander my name.

Do thou our Moses' sacred laws disgrace,
Deprave our nation, do me some despite.
I'm apt enough to fight in any case,
But yet for Salome I will not fight.

SILLEUS

Nor I for aught but Salome. My sword,   25
That owes his service to her sacred name,
Will not an edge for other cause afford –
In other fight, I am not sure of fame.

CONSTABARUS

For her, I pity thee enough already.
For her, I therefore will not mangle thee.   30
A woman with a heart so most unsteady
Will, of herself, sufficient torture be.
I cannot envy for so light a gain –
Her mind with such unconstancy doth run,
As, with a word, thou didst her love obtain,   35
So, with a word, she will from thee be won –
So light as her possession 's, for most day
Is her affection lost: to me 'tis known.
As good go hold the wind as make her stay –
She never loves, but till she call her own.   40
She merely is a painted sepulchre,
That is both fair and vilely foul at once;
Though on her outside graces garnish her,
Her mind is filled with worse than rotten bones,
And ever ready lifted is her hand   45
To aim destruction at a husband's throat.
For proofs, Josephus and myself do stand,
Though once on both of us she seemed to dote.

---

22   *Deprave* Defame.
28   i.e. Silleus will not win renown by fighting for any cause but Salome's good name.
29   *For* Because of.
37–8 These lines are obscure, but seem to refer back to 'light' at l. 33. Constabarus cannot
      envy Silleus for so light a possession as Salome, because he knows her affections
      change most days.
37   *possession 's* ed. (possessions Q).
38   *affection* ed. (affections Q).
39   Proverbial (Tilley, W416). Compare 'Sithens in a net I seek to hold the wind' in Sir
      Thomas Wyatt's sonnet, 'Whoso list to hunt'.
40   i.e. She only loves what she can control as her own.
41–4 *painted . . . bones* See Matthew 23.27.

Her mouth, though serpent-like it never hisses,
Yet like a serpent, poisons where it kisses.   50

SILLEUS
Well, Hebrew, well! Thou bark'st, but wilt not bite.

CONSTABARUS
I tell thee still for her I will not fight.

SILLEUS
Why, then I call thee coward.

CONSTABARUS   From my heart,
I give thee thanks. A coward's hateful name
Cannot to valiant minds a blot impart,   55
And therefore I with joy receive the same.
Thou know'st I am no coward: thou wert by
At the Arabian battle th' other day
And saw'st my sword with daring valiancy
Amongst the faint Arabians cut my way.   60
The blood of foes no more could let it shine
And 'twas enamellèd with some of thine.

                                    [*Draws his sword*]

But now, have at thee! Not for Salome
I fight, but to discharge a coward's style.
Here 'gins the fight that shall not parted be   65
Before a soul or two endure exile.

                    [*They fight*]

SILLEUS
Thy sword hath made some windows for my blood   ] *wounded*
To show a horrid, crimson phys'nomy.
To breathe for both of us methinks 'twere good –
The day will give us time enough to die.   70

CONSTABARUS
With all my heart, take breath. Thou shalt have time,
And if thou list, a twelvemonth. Let us end.
Into thy cheeks there doth a paleness climb –

---

57   *by* present.
58   *Arabian battle* For Josephus's account of Herod's wars against the Arabians, see
     Ant., 15.6.390ff.
64   *style* name.
66   *endure exile* are parted from their bodies: compare I.iv.3 above.
68   *phys'nomy* face: see II.ii.102n. above.
69   *To breathe* To rest.

Thou canst not from my sword thyself defend.
What needest thou for Salome to fight?   75
Thou hast her and may'st keep her – none strives for her.
I willingly to thee resign my right,
For in my very soul I do abhor her.
Thou see'st that I am fresh, unwounded yet.
Then not for fear, I do this offer make: 80
Thou art with loss of blood, to fight unfit,
For here is one, and there another take.

SILLEUS

I will not leave as long as breath remains
Within my wounded body – spare your words.
My heart, in blood's stead, courage entertains –   85
Salome's love no place for fear affords.

CONSTABARUS

Oh, could thy soul but prophesy like mine,
I would not wonder thou should'st long to die,
For Salome, if I aright divine,
Will be than death a greater misery.   90

SILLEUS

Then, list: I'll breathe no longer.

CONSTABARUS   Do thy will:

I hateless fight and charitably kill. Ay, ay!

They fight

Pity thyself, Silleus. Let not death
Intrude before his time into thy heart.
Alas, it is too late to fear: his breath   95
Is from his body now about to part.
How farest thou brave Arabian?

SILLEUS   Very well.

My leg is hurt; I can no longer fight.
It only grieves me that so soon I fell
Before fair Salom's wrongs I came to right.   100

---

82   i.e. For here is one wound, and there (in a further fight) you will receive another.
91   *list* listen.
      breathe rest, with an additional meaning of 'live'.
92   *Ay, ay! / They fight* ed. (I, I, they fight Q). A stage direction appears to have been set
      as speech here, and Constabarus's apparent exclamation, 'I, I', might be a
      compositor's mistake.
100   *came to* was able to.

CONSTABARUS

Thy wounds are less than mortal. Never fear –
Thou shalt a safe and quick recovery find.
Come, I will thee unto my lodging bear –
I hate thy body, but I love thy mind.

SILLEUS

Thanks, noble Jew. I see a courteous foe.   105
Stern enmity to friendship can no art –
Had not my heart and tongue engaged me so,
I would from thee no foe, but friend, depart.
My heart to Salome is tied so fast
To leave her love for friendship, yet my skill   110
Shall be employed to make your favour last
And I will honour Constabarus still.

CONSTABARUS

I ope my bosom to thee and will take
Thee in as friend and grieve for thy complaint,
But if we do not expedition make,   115
Thy loss of blood, I fear, will make thee faint.

              [*Exeunt* CONSTABARUS *with* SILLEUS]

[CHORUS]

CHORUS

To hear a tale with ears prejudicate,
It spoils the judgement and corrupts the sense.
That human error given to every state
Is greater enemy to innocence: 120
    It makes us foolish, heady, rash, unjust;
    It makes us never try before we trust.

101   *mortal* fatal.
106   i.e. Enmity knows no way to become friendship.
109   *so* Many editors emend to 'too', but the line makes sense as it stands.
115   *expedition* haste.
117   *prejudicate* affected by preconceived opinion.
118   *judgement* See II.i.29n. above.
119   *state* type or rank of person.
120   i.e. The innocent or uneducated are very susceptible to false rumour. This
       statement resonates with Pheroras's approval of Graphina's intelligence, and
       Salome's riposte: see III.i.124–7 below.
122   *try . . . trust* make sure something is true before we trust it. Proverbial: see Tilley,
       T595.

It will confound the meaning, change the words,
For it our sense of hearing much deceives –
Besides, no time to judgement it affords,   125
To weigh the circumstance our ear receives.
    The ground of accidents it never tries,
    But makes us take for truth ten thousand lies.

Our ears and hearts are apt to hold for good
That we ourselves do most desire to be,   130
And then we drown objections in the flood
Of partiality. 'Tis that we see
    That makes false rumours long with credit passed,
    Though they like rumours must conclude at last.

The greatest part of us, prejudicate   135
With wishing Herod's death, do hold it true –
The being once deluded doth not bate
The credit to a better likelihood due.
    Those few that wish it not, the multitude
    Do carry headlong, so they doubts conclude.   140

They not object the weak, uncertain ground
Whereon they built this tale of Herod's end,
Whereof the author scarcely can be found,
And all because their wishes that way bend.
    They think not of the peril that ensu'th   145
    If this should prove the contrary to truth.

---

123   *confound* corrupt.
127   i.e. It [human error] never tests or explores the reasons behind incidental occurrences.
130   *That* That which.
132   *that* that partiality.
133   i.e. That gives false rumours credit for a long time.
135   *us* The Chorus's use of 'us' here moves from the general to the particular, indicating the desires of the 'company of Jews', as well as, by implication, those of the play's readers.
137–8   i.e. Being deluded once does not stop people giving credit to things they think are likely.
140   *conclude* overcome (*OED, conclude v.* 4).
141   *They* The few.
142   *they* the multitude.

On this same doubt, on this so light a breath,
They pawn their lives and fortunes, for they all
Behave them as the news of Herod's death
They did of most undoubted credit call: 150
    But if their actions now do rightly hit,
    Let them commend their fortune, not their wit.

---

147   *light a breath* Compare with Constabarus's evocation of Salome's lightness at
       II.iv.33–9: lightness and inconstancy are dangerous.
151   *rightly hit* hit the mark.
152   *commend* thank.
       wit The discourse on 'wit' is taken up by Constabarus in the next scene when he
       reveals it was Graphina's mind, more than her beauty, that attracted him.

ACT III, SCENE i

[Enter] PHERORAS *[and]* SALOME

PHERORAS
Urge me no more Graphina to forsake.
Not twelve hours since, I married her for love,
And do you think a sister's power can make
A resolute decree so soon remove?

SALOME
Poor minds they are that honour not affects.   5

PHERORAS
Who hunts for honour, happiness neglects.

SALOME
You might have been both of felicity
And honour, too, in equal measure seized.

PHERORAS
It is not you can tell so well as I
What 'tis can make me happy or displeased.   10

SALOME
To match for neither beauty nor respects,
One mean of birth, but yet of meaner mind,
A woman full of natural defects –
I wonder what your eye in her could find.

PHERORAS
Mine eye found loveliness, mine ear found wit,   15
To please the one and to enchant the other.
Grace on her eye, mirth on her tongue, doth sit;
In looks a child, in wisdom's house a mother.

SALOME
But say you thought her fair, as none thinks else,
Knows not Pheroras, beauty is a blast,   20
Much like this flower which today excels,

---

0   s.d. ed. (Actus tertius: Scoena prima. Q).
5   Compare Salome's words at I.iv.21–8.
8   *seized* possessed.
11 *respects* rank.
12 *mean* low.
20 *blast* brief explosive gust. Lines 21–2 develop the simile to encompass the meaning
    of 'a blasted bud or blossom' (see *OED*, *blast n*.1, 7).

51

But longer than a day it will not last?

PHERORAS
Her wit exceeds her beauty.

SALOME   Wit may show
The way to ill as well as good, you know.

PHERORAS
But wisdom is the porter of her head,   25
And bars all wicked words from issuing thence.

SALOME
But of a porter, better were you sped,
If she against their entrance made defence.

*[trying to
to confirm]*

[*Enter* ANANELL]

PHERORAS
But wherefore comes the sacred Ananell,
That hitherward his hasty steps doth bend?   30
[*To* ANANELL] Great sacrificer, y' are arrivèd well –
Ill news from holy mouth I not attend.

ACT III, SCENE ii

PHERORAS, SALOME [*and*] ANANELL

ANANELL
My lips, my son, with peaceful tidings blest,
Shall utter honey to your listening ear.

*[a priest
figure?]*

A word of death comes not from priestly breast.
I speak of life; in life there is no fear.
And for the news, I did the heavens salute   5
And filled the temple with my thankful voice,

---

25 *porter* door keeper.
26 *bars* prevents.
27 *better . . . sped* you would be better served.
31 *sacrificer* See III.ii.16 below.
32 *I not attend* I do not expect.

 0 ed. (Actus tertius. Scoena 2. Q).

For though that mourning may not me pollute,
At pleasing accidents I may rejoice.

PHERORAS

Is Herod then revived from certain death?

SALOME

What? Can your news restore my brother's breath?   10

ANANELL

Both so, and so. The king is safe and sound,
And did such grace in royal Caesar meet
That he, with larger style than ever crowned,
Within this hour, Jerusalem will greet.
I did but come to tell you and must back   15
To make preparatives for sacrifice.
I knew his death your hearts like mine did rack,
Though to conceal it, provèd you wise.   [*Exit*]

SALOME

How can my joy sufficiently appear?

PHERORAS

A heavier tale did never pierce mine ear.   20

SALOME

Now Salome of happiness may boast.

PHERORAS

But now Pheroras is in danger most.

SALOME

I shall enjoy the comfort of my life.

PHERORAS

And I shall lose it, losing of my wife.

SALOME

Joy, heart, for Constabarus shall be slain.   25

PHERORAS

Grieve, soul; Graphina shall from me be ta'en.

SALOME

Smile, cheeks; the fair Silleus shall be mine.

contrast in react

---

  7 *mourning . . . pollute* God told Moses that priests should have limited contact with
     the dead: see Leviticus 21.1–4.
 13 *larger style* greater title.
 17 *rack* torment.
19–28 Cary's use of stychomythia here underlines the stark differences between Salome's
     and Pheroras's reactions to Ananell's news.

PHERORAS

Weep, eyes, for I must with a child combine.

SALOME

Well, brother, cease your moans. On one condition
I'll undertake to win the king's consent;   30
Graphina still shall be in your tuition,
And her with you be ne'ertheless content.

PHERORAS

What's the condition? Let me quickly know,
That I as quickly your command may act,
Were it to see what herbs in Ophir grow,   35
Or that the lofty Tyrus might be sacked.

SALOME

'Tis not so hard a task: it is no more
But tell the king that Constabarus hid
The sons of Baba, done to death before,
And 'tis no more than Constabarus did.   40
And tell him more, that he, for Herod's sake,
Not able to endure his brother's foe,
Did with a bill our separation make,
Though loath from Constabarus else to go.

PHERORAS

Believe this tale for told. I'll go from hence,   45
In Herod's ear the Hebrew to deface,
And I, that never studied eloquence,
Do mean with eloquence this tale to grace.   *Exit*

SALOME

This will be Constabarus' quick dispatch,
Which, from my mouth, would lesser credit find.   50
Yet shall he not decease without a match,

---

28   *combine* couple, unite.
31   *tuition* protection, custody.
35   *Ophir* Biblical region, famous for its wealth: see, for example, 1 Kings 9.28.
36   *Tyrus* Tyre, a Phoenician coastal city, rich in trade: see 1 Maccabees 11.59.
      sacked plundered.
37   *not* ed. (no Q).
39   *done to death* doomed to death.
41–2 *he, his* Weller and Ferguson emend to 'we' and 'our', while Hodgson-Wright prefers
      'I' and 'our'. Salome could, though, be instructing Pheroras to pretend he was the
      instigator of the divorce, thereby concealing her own actions: see l. 50 below.
49   *dispatch* killing, execution.

For Mariam shall not linger long behind.
First, jealousy – if that avail not, fear –
Shall be my minister to work her end:
A common error moves not Herod's ear   55
Which doth so firmly to his Mariam bend.
She shall be chargèd with so horrid crime   *plotting*
As Herod's fear shall turn his love to hate –
I'll make some swear that she desires to climb
And seeks to poison him for his estate.   60
I scorn that she should live my birth t'upbraid,
To call me base and hungry Edomite;
With patient show her choler I betrayed,   *bitterness anger*
And watched the time to be revenged by sleight.
Now, tongue of mine, with scandal load her name,   65
Turn hers to fountains, Herod's eyes to flame.
Yet first I will begin Pheroras' suit
That he my earnest business may effect,
And I of Mariam will keep me mute
Till first some other doth her name detect.   70

[*Enter* SERVANT]

Who's there? Silleus' man? How fares your lord
That your aspects do bear the badge of sorrow?
SILLEUS' MAN
He hath the marks of Constabarus' sword
And for a while desires your sight to borrow.
SALOME
My heavy curse the hateful sword pursue;   75
My heavier curse on the more hateful arm

---

55   i.e. Herod won't be swayed against Mariam by the report of a common
      misdemeanour.
59   *climb* elevate herself.
60   *estate* kingdom and position. Compare *Hamlet*, 'A poisons him i'th' garden for 's
      estate' (III.ii.239).
63   Salome seems to believe she patiently led Mariam to reveal her anger. It is likely
      that this refers back to I.iii.17–24.
64   *sleight* cunning.
67   *begin . . . suit* plead Pheroras's cause (before Herod).
70   *detect* expose.
72   *aspects* looks.
74   i.e. And wishes to see you for a while.

That wounded my Silleus. But renew
Your tale again: hath he no mortal harm?

SILLEUS' MAN
No sign of danger doth in him appear,
Nor are his wounds in place of peril seen.   80
He bids you be assured you need not fear –
He hopes to make you yet Arabia's queen.

SALOME
Commend my heart to be Silleus' charge.
Tell him my brother's sudden coming now
Will give my foot no room to walk at large,   85
But I will see him yet ere night, I vow.

[*Exeunt*]

ACT III, SCENE iii

[*Enter*] MARIAM *and* SOHEMUS

MARIAM
Sohemus, tell me what the news may be
That makes your eyes so full, your cheeks so blue?

SOHEMUS
I know not how to call them. Ill for me,
'Tis sure they are; not so, I hope, for you.
Herod –

MARIAM   Oh, what of Herod?

SOHEMUS   Herod lives.   5

[MARIAM]
How! Lives? What, in some cave or forest hid?

SOHEMUS
Nay, back returned with honour. Caesar gives
Him greater grace than e'er Antonius did.

---

78   *mortal harm* fatal wound.
83   i.e. Tell Silleus, my heart is in his possession.

0   s.d. ed. (Actus 3. Scoena 3. Q).
2   *blue* i.e. bloodless.
3   *them* the news, imagined as plural.

MARIAM

    Foretell the ruin of my family,

    Tell me that I shall see our city burned,   10

    Tell me I shall a death disgraceful die,

    But tell me not that Herod is returned.

SOHEMUS

    Be not impatient, madam; be but mild –

    His love to you again will soon be bred.

MARIAM

    I will not to his love be reconciled;   15

    With solemn vows I have forsworn his bed.

SOHEMUS

    But you must break those vows.

MARIAM   I'll rather break

    The heart of Mariam. Cursed is my fate.

    But speak no more to me; in vain ye speak

    To live with him I so profoundly hate.   20

SOHEMUS

    Great queen, you must to me your pardon give;

    Sohemus cannot now your will obey.

    If your command should me to silence drive,

    It were not to obey, but to betray.

    Reject and slight my speeches, mock my faith,   25

    Scorn my observance, call my counsel nought,

    Though you regard not what Sohemus saith

    Yet will I ever freely speak my thought.

    I fear ere long I shall fair Mariam see

    In woeful state and by herself undone.   30

    Yet for your issue's sake, more temp'rate be –

    The heart by affability is won.

MARIAM

    And must I to my prison turn again?

    Oh, now I see I was an hypocrite;

    I did this morning for his death complain,   35

19–20   *in . . . hate* you urge me in vain to live with him I hate so deeply.

23–4   Sohemus asserts that obedient silence is sometimes tantamount to betrayal. See
       Introduction for a discussion of how this conundrum is presented in the play.

26   *nought* nothing.

28   This is ironic, for it is also Mariam's problem: see, especially, l. 65 below.

31   *issue's* children's.

35–6   Cary here foregrounds the play's adherence to the classical unity of time.

And yet do mourn, because he lives ere night.
When I his death believed, compassion wrought
And was the stickler 'twixt my heart and him,
But now that curtain's drawn from off my thought,
Hate doth appear again with visage grim   40
And paints the face of Herod in my heart
In horrid colours with detested look.
Then fear would come, but scorn doth play her part
And saith that scorn with fear can never brook.
I know I could enchain him with a smile   45
And lead him captive with a gentle word –
I scorn my look should ever man beguile,
Or other speech than meaning to afford.
Else Salome in vain might spend her wind,
In vain might Herod's mother whet her tongue,   50
In vain had they complotted and combined,
For I could overthrow them all ere long.
Oh, what a shelter is mine innocence,
To shield me from the pangs of inward grief.
'Gainst all mishaps it is my fair defence   55
And to my sorrows yields a large relief.
To be commandress of the triple earth
And sit in safety from a fall secure,
To have all nations celebrate my birth,
I would not that my spirit were impure.   60
Let my distressèd state unpitied be:
Mine innocence is hope enough for me.   *Exit*

SOHEMUS

Poor guiltless queen. Oh, that my wish might place
A little temper now about thy heart.
Unbridled speech is Mariam's worst disgrace,   65

---

38   *stickler* moderator.
44   *brook* tolerate (each other).
48   i.e. Or suggest any interpretation other than my true meaning.
49   *wind* breath.
50   *Herod's mother* Cypros. Josephus notes she plotted with her daughter, Salome, against Mariam: see *Ant.*, 15.11.398–9.
57   *triple earth* the empire ruled by the Roman triumvirate.
60   Compare with Salome's completely opposite sentiments at I.iv.21–34 above.
64   *temper* moderation.
65   Josephus, too, notes Mariam was too liberal in her speech: see *Ant.*, 15.11.398–9.

And will endanger her without desert.
I am in greater hazard – o'er my head
The fatal axe doth hang unsteadily.
My disobedience, once discoverèd,
Will shake it down; Sohemus so shall die.   70
For when the king shall find we thought his death
Had been as certain as we see his life,
And marks withal I slighted so his breath
As to preserve alive his matchless wife –
Nay more, to give to Alexander's hand   75
The regal dignity, the sovereign power;
How I had yielded up, at her command,
The strength of all the city, David's tower –
What more than common death may I expect,
Since I too well do know his cruelty.   80
'Twere death, a word of Herod's to neglect:
What, then, to do directly contrary?
Yet, life, I quit thee with a willing spirit,
And think thou could'st not better be employed.
I forfeit thee for her that more doth merit;   85
Ten such were better dead than she destroyed.
But fare thee well, chaste queen, well may I see
The darkness palpable and rivers part,
The sun stand still – nay, more, retorted be –
But never woman with so pure a heart.   90
Thine eyes' grave majesty keeps all in awe
And cuts the wings of every loose desire,

---

66   *desert* merit, deserving.
68   *fatal axe* the sword of Damocles, but, as Purkiss notes, this also alludes to the
      means by which the early modern nobility were executed and prefigures Mariam's
      death.
73   *breath* commandment.
75   *Alexander's* Hodgson-Wright and others emend to 'Alexandra's', but it seems more
      likely that Sohemus would pass regnal power to Alexander, son of Herod and
      Mariam, mentioned at I.ii.62 above. See also IV.iv.49–50 below.
78   *David's tower* Anachronistic. The name was adopted during the Ottoman empire
      to refer to fortifications initially built by Herod on the Western Hill of Jerusalem.
83–96 Bell calls this a 'perfect sonnet soliloquy' that idealises Mariam's virtue and
      foregrounds Sohemus's undying, unrequited love (Bell, 29).
86   *such* lives such as mine.
88–9 *darkness . . . still* A reference to Moses's parting of the Red Sea: see Exodus 14.19–22.
89   *retorted* cast back. This is a reference to Joshua 10.12–14 where Joshua commanded
      the sun to stand still.

Thy brow is table to the modest law,
Yet though we dare not love, we may admire.
And, if I die, it shall my soul content,   95
My breath in Mariam's service shall be spent.   [*Exit*]

couthley lawe/devotion?

[CHORUS]

CHORUS

'Tis not enough for one that is a wife
To keep her spotless from an act of ill,
But from suspicion she should free her life
And bare herself of power as well as will.
    'Tis not so glorious for her to be free,   100
    As by her proper self restrained to be.

women should be restrain

When she hath spacious ground to walk upon,
Why on the ridge should she desire to go?
It is no glory to forbear alone
Those things that may her honour overthrow.   105
    But 'tis thank-worthy if she will not take
    All lawful liberties for honour's sake.

That wife her hand against her fame doth rear
That more than to her lord alone will give
A private word to any second ear,   110
And though she may with reputation live,

---

93   *table* tablet (on which the law is written). Compare Exodus 34.1.
      modest law Purkiss suggests this means the 'law of modesty'. However, it also
      implies a temperate, non-domineering law.
97   s.p. This Chorus, unlike the others in the play, does not use the first-person plural.
      Bell suggests it is made up of men who think they have the right to control their
      wives (Bell, 30).
99   *from . . . life* Shell notes an analogous sentiment in the *Life*: 'She did always
      disapprove the practice of satisfying one's self with their conscience being free from
      fault, not forbearing all that might have the least show' (Alison Shell, 'Elizabeth
      Cary's historical conscience: *The Tragedy of Mariam* and Thomas Lodge's Josephus',
      The Literary Career and Legacy of Elizabeth Cary, 1613–1680, ed. Heather Wolfe
      (2007), pp. 53–67, p. 57). This sentiment also appears in conduct manuals: Weller
      and Ferguson cite Stefano Guazzo's *Civil Conversation*, trans. Pettie and Yong
      (1581–6): 'It is not sufficient to be honest and innocent in deed, if she do not like-
      wise avoid all suspicion'.
100 *bare* strip, with a possible meaning of 'bar', as in 'prevent herself from having
      power'.
102 *proper* own.
105 *alone* only.

Yet though most chaste, she doth her glory blot
And wounds her honour, though she kills it not.

When to their husbands they themselves do bind,
Do they not wholly give themselves away?   115
Or give they but their body, not their mind,
Reserving that, though best, for others' prey?
   No, sure, their thoughts no more can be their own,
   And therefore should to none but one be known.

                                           120
Then she usurps upon another's right
That seeks to be by public language graced,
And though her thoughts reflect with purest light,
Her mind, if not peculiar, is not chaste.
   For in a wife it is no worse to find
   A common body, than a common mind.   125

And every mind, though free from thought of ill,
That out of glory seeks a worth to show
When any's ears but one therewith they fill,
Doth, in a sort, her pureness overthrow.
   Now Mariam had – but that to this she bent –   130
   Been free from fear as well as innocent.

chorus meditating on

115–20   The Chorus invoke the legal doctrine of *couverture* which sees the husband and
           wife as one mind and body under the jurisdiction of the man (see Introduction).
   121   *another's* i.e. her husband's.
   124   *peculiar* one person's private property.
   126   *common body* i.e. one that is prostituted.
   128   *out of glory* out of a desire for fame.
   131   *she bent* she was inclined (to speak liberally).

ACT IV, SCENE i

Enter HEROD *and his* ATTENDANTS

HEROD
Hail, happy city; happy in thy store,
And happy that thy buildings such we see.
More happy in the temple where w' adore,
But most of all that Mariam lives in thee.

[*Enter* NUNTIO]

[*To* NUNTIO] Art thou returned? How fares my Mariam?   5
NUNTIO
She's well, my lord, and will anon be here
As you commanded.
HEROD   Muffle up thy brow
Thou day's dark taper; Mariam will appear
And where she shines we need not thy dim light.
Oh, haste thy steps, rare creature, speed thy pace   10
And let thy presence make the day more bright,
And cheer the heart of Herod with thy face.
It is an age since I from Mariam went –
Methinks our parting was in David's days,
The hours are so increased by discontent;   15
Deep sorrow, Joshua-like, the season stays.
But when I am with Mariam, time runs on;
Her sight can make months minutes, days of weeks,
An hour is then no sooner come than gone

---

0   s.d. ed. (Actus quartus: Scoena prima. Q).
1   *store* abundance.
2   *such* of the like.
4   s.d. After l. 5 in Q.
6   *anon* immediately.
7–8   *Muffle . . . taper* Herod begins to use the language of love poetry, observing that
      Mariam's beauty eclipses the sun's light.
14   *David's days* the time of the biblical King David. Weller and Ferguson suggest this
      was roughly a thousand years previously.
16   *Joshua-like . . . stays* In Joshua 10.12–14, Joshua commanded the sun to stand still.
      Compare Sohemus's image at III.iii.89.
18   *Her sight* The sight of her.

When in her face mine eye for wonders seeks.   20
You world-commanding city, Europe's grace,
Twice hath my curious eye your streets surveyed,
And I have seen the statue-fillèd place
That once, if not for geese, had been betrayed.
I all your Roman beauties have beheld,   25
And seen the shows your Aediles did prepare;
I saw the sum of what in you excelled,
Yet saw no miracle like Mariam rare.
The fair and famous Livia, Caesar's love,
The world's commanding mistress, did I see,   30
Whose beauties both the world and Rome approve –
Yet Mariam, Livia is not like to thee.
Be patient but a little while, mine eyes;
Within your compassed limits be contained;
That object straight shall your desires suffice   35
From which you were so long a while restrained.
How wisely Mariam doth the time delay,
Lest sudden joy my sense should suffocate.
I am prepared. Thou need'st no longer stay.

[*Someone approaches*]

Who's there? My Mariam? More than happy fate!   40
Oh, no – it is Pheroras. Welcome, brother.
Now for a while, I must my passion smother.

21   *world-commanding city* Rome.
23   *the statue-fillèd place* the Capitol.
24   *geese* ed. (griefe Q). Dunstan and Greg first suggested this emendation. It refers to
      the tale of the Capitoline geese, told by Livy, which were supposed to have
      awakened the Romans when the Gauls attempted a surprise night-time attack,
      c. 390 BCE. It is possible, though, that Q's 'griefe' refers back to Caesar's grief over
      Pompey's death, mentioned by Mariam at I.i.3–4.
26   *Aediles* Roman magistrates in charge of municipal shows.
29   *Livia* Livia Drusilla, whose marital story resonates with that of Mariam. She was
      the second wife of Octavius Caesar, marrying him after they had both divorced
      their first spouses. Nevertheless, Herod insists that Livia and Mariam are not alike:
      l. 32 below.
33–4 Herod addresses an apostrophe to his eyes.
34   *compassed* circumscribed.
35   Herod tells his eyes that Mariam ('That object') will soon satisfy their desires (to
      see her).

63

ACT IV, SCENE ii

[*Enter to*] HEROD, PHERORAS

PHERORAS

    All health and safety wait upon my lord,
    And may you long in prosperous fortunes live
    With Rome-commanding Caesar at accord,
    And have all honours that the world can give.

HEROD

    Oh, brother, now thou speak'st not from thy heart.   5
    No, thou hast struck a blow at Herod's love
    That cannot quickly from my memory part
    Though Salome did me to pardon move.
    Valiant Phasaelus, now to thee farewell;
    Thou wert my kind and honourable brother.   10
    Oh, hapless hour, when you self-stricken fell,
    Thou father's image, glory of thy mother.
    Had I desired a greater suit of thee
    Than to withhold thee from a harlot's bed
    Thou would'st have granted it, but now I see   15
    All are not like that in a womb are bred.
    Thou wouldst not, had'st thou heard of Herod's death,
    Have made his burial time thy bridal hour.
    Thou wouldst with clamours, not with joyful breath,
    Have showed the news to be not sweet, but sour.   20

PHERORAS

    Phasaelus' great worth I know did stain
    Pheroras' petty valour, but they lie
    (Excepting you, yourself) that dare maintain
    That he did honour Herod more than I,
    For what I showed, love's power constrained me show,   25
    And pardon loving faults for Mariam's sake.

    0   s.d. ed. (Actus quartus. Scoena secunda. Q).
    3   *at accord* in agreement, harmony.
    9   *Phasaelus* Herod and Pheroras's brother. He knocked his brains out on a stone
          rather than be executed by his enemies: see *Ant.*, 14.25.373.
   16   *like* alike. Phasaelus and Pheroras had the same mother.
   21   The line is metrically irregular, unless 'Phasaelus' (unlike in l. 9 above) is quatro-
          syllabic.

HEROD

    Mariam! Where is she?

PHERORAS   Nay, I do not know,

    But absent use of her fair name I make.

    You have forgiven greater faults than this,

    For Constabarus, that against your will   30

    Preserved the sons of Baba, lives in bliss,

    Though you commanded him the youths to kill. *con Fessing*

HEROD

    Go: take a present order for his death

    And let those traitors feel the worst of fears.

    Now Salome will whine to beg his breath,   35

    But I'll be deaf to prayers and blind to tears.

PHERORAS

    He is, my lord, from Salome divorced,

    Though her affection did to leave him grieve,

    Yet was she, by her love to you, enforced

    To leave the man that would your foes relieve.   40

HEROD

    Then haste them to their death. I will requite

    Thee, gentle Mariam – Salom, I mean.

    The thought of Mariam doth so steal my spirit

    My mouth from speech of her I cannot wean.

Exit [PHERORAS]

---

29   Pheroras pretends Herod knows about, and has forgiven, Constabarus's disobedi-
       ence.

30   *your* ed. (you Q).

35   *whine* Herod's verb choice reveals his low opinion of Salome's supplications. See
       also IV.vii.105n. below.

37   *Salome* ed. (*Salom* Q).

38–9   Pheroras's syntax separates Salome's 'affection' for Constabarus from her loving
       duty to Herod, showing the latter to be most compelling.

42   *Salom* Cary truncates Salome's name to maintain the iambic pentameter.

ACT IV, SCENE iii

[*Enter to*] HEROD, MARIAM

HEROD

And here she comes, indeed. Happily met
My best and dearest half. What ails my dear?
Thou dost the difference certainly forget
'Twixt dusky habits and a time so clear.

MARIAM

My lord, I suit my garment to my mind   5
And there no cheerful colours can I find.

HEROD

Is this my welcome? Have I longed so much
To see my dearest Mariam discontent?
What is't that is the cause thy heart to touch?
Oh, speak, that I thy sorrow may prevent.   10
Art thou not Jewry's queen and Herod's, too?
Be my commandress, be my sovereign guide –
To be by thee directed, I will woo,
For in thy pleasure lies my highest pride.
Or if thou think Judea's narrow bound   15
Too strict a limit for thy great command,
Thou shalt be empress of Arabia crowned,
For thou shalt rule and I will win the land.
I'll rob the holy David's sepulchre
To give thee wealth, if thou for wealth do care;   20
Thou shalt have all they did with him inter,
And I for thee will make the temple bare.

MARIAM

I neither have of power nor riches want.

---

  0   s.d. ed. (Actus 4. Scoena 3. Q).
  4   *dusky habits* dark clothes.
       clear joyful, with a sense of sunny weather.
7–8   These lines, and the scene as a whole, are inspired by *Ant.*, 15.11.396–7.
 12   *commandress . . . sovereign guide* While Herod's language might recall that of
      Petrarchan love poetry, it also shows he is unnaturally in thrall to his wife.
 19   *holy David's sepulchre* Sometime after Mariam's death, Herod is reputed to have
      opened David's tomb: see *Ant.*, 16.11.423. This episode is adjacent to Josephus's
      description of Pheroras's marriage, so might have been on Cary's mind at the time.
 23   i.e. I do not have have need of power, neither do I desire riches.

I have enough, nor do I wish for more.
Your offers to my heart no ease can grant   25
Except they could my brother's life restore.
No: had you wished the wretched Mariam glad,
Or had your love to her been truly tied –
Nay, had you not desired to make her sad –
My brother nor my grandsire had not died.   30

HEROD

Wilt thou believe no oaths to clear thy lord?
How oft have I with execration sworn
Thou art by me beloved, by me adored?
Yet are my protestations heard with scorn.
Hircanus plotted to deprive my head   35
Of this long-settled honour that I wear,
And therefore I did justly doom him dead
To rid the realm from peril, me from fear.
Yet I, for Mariam's sake, do so repent
The death of one, whose blood she did inherit,   40
I wish I had a kingdom's treasure spent
So I had ne'er expelled Hircanus' spirit.
As I affected that same noble youth,
In lasting infamy my name enroll
If I not mourned his death with hearty truth.   45
Did I not show to him my earnest love
When I to him the priesthood did restore,
And did for him a living priest remove,
Which never had been done but once before?

MARIAM

I know that, moved by importunity,   50
You made him priest and shortly after die.

---

32   *execration* This usually means 'cursing' but, as Weller and Ferguson note, the Latin
     exsecratio can mean either a 'curse' or an 'oath with an imprecation'.
35   *Hircanus* Mariam's grandfather, killed by Herod. See *Ant.*, 15.9.394, for an account
     of his death.
36   *long-settled honour* crown.
37   *justly* rightly, but also with a sense of legally.
42   Most editors suggest a line of verse is missing between ll. 42–3. The syntax is
     corrupted and 'enroll' at l. 44 has no rhyme.
43   *affected* felt affection towards.
     noble youth Aristobolus, Mariam's brother.
49   *done . . . before* See *Ant.*, 15.3.385. Joesphus explains that before Herod replaced
     Ananell with Aristobolus, Antiochus Epiphanes replaced Josuah with Onias.

HEROD

I will not speak, unless to be believed.
This froward humour will not do you good –
It hath too much already Herod grieved
To think that you on terms of hate have stood.   55
Yet smile, my dearest Mariam, do but smile,
And I will all unkind conceits exile.

MARIAM

I cannot frame disguise, nor never taught
My face a look dissenting from my thought.

HEROD

By heaven, you vex me. Build not on my love.   60

MARIAM

I will not build on so unstable ground.

HEROD

Naught is so fixed, but peevishness may move.

MARIAM

'Tis better slightest cause than none were found.

HEROD

Be judge, yourself, if ever Herod sought,
Or would be moved, a cause of change to find.   65
Yet let your look declare a milder thought,
My heart again you shall to Mariam bind.
How oft did I for you my mother chide,
Revile my sister and my brother rate,
And tell them all my Mariam they belied?   70
Distrust me still, if these be signs of hate.

---

53   *froward* perverse. (Compare IV.vi.55 below.)
57   *conceits* thoughts.
58   *frame* fashion or construct.
58–9 Compare III.iii.47–8 above.
60   *Build not* Do not rely.
61   See Matthew 7.26–7.
62   i.e. Nothing is so fixed that (your) petty bad temper won't change it (with an
      additional sense of 'move (Herod) to anger').
69   *rate* scold.
70   *belied* misrepresented.

ACT IV, SCENE iv

[*Enter* BUTLER]

HEROD

What hast thou here?

BUTLER   A drink procuring love.

The queen desired me to deliver it.

MARIAM

Did I? Some hateful practice this will prove,

Yet can it be no worse than heavens permit.

HEROD

Confess the truth, thou wicked instrument   5

To her outrageous will. 'Tis poison, sure.

Tell true and thou shalt 'scape the punishment,

Which, if thou do conceal, thou shalt endure.

BUTLER

I know not, but I doubt it be no less.

Long since the hate of you her heart did seize.   10

HEROD

Know'st thou the cause thereof?

BUTLER   My lord, I guess:

Sohemus told the tale that did displease.

HEROD

Oh, heaven! Sohemus false! Go let him die:

Stay not to suffer him to speak a word.

[*Exit* BUTLER]

Oh, damnèd villain, did he falsify   15

The oath he swore e'en of his own accord?

Now do I know thy falsehood, painted devil,

Thou white enchantress. Oh, thou art so foul

---

   0   s.d. ed. (Actus 4. Scoena 4. Q).

  1–2   The Butler's actions are directly inspired by *Ant.*, 15.11.398.

   3   *practice* plot.

   6   *poison* ed. (passion Q). Dunstan and Greg first emended to 'poison'. It is possible
        that Herod asks the Butler whether the drink provokes passion. However, the
        Butler's reply at l. 9 makes more sense if Herod asks if the cup contains poison.

  10   *seize* ed. (cease Q).

 17–18 *painted . . . enchantress* Compare II.iv.41–4. A Renaissance proverb maintained 'the
        white devil is worse than the black' (Tilley, D310).

That hyssop cannot cleanse thee, worst of evil –
A beauteous body hides a loathsome soul.   20
Your love, Sohemus, moved by his affection,
Though he have ever heretofore been true,
Did blab, forsooth, that I did give direction,
If we were put to death, to slaughter you.
And you, in black revenge, attended now   25
To add a murder to your breach of vow.

MARIAM
  Is this a dream?

HEROD   Oh, heaven, that 'twere no more.
  I'll give my realm to who can prove it so.
  I would I were like any beggar poor,
  So I for false my Mariam did not know.   30
  Foul pith containèd in the fairest rind
  That ever graced a cedar. Oh, thine eye
  Is pure as heaven, but impure thy mind,
  And for impurity shall Mariam die.
  Why didst thou love Sohemus?

MARIAM   They can tell   35
  That say I loved him: Mariam says not so.

HEROD
  Oh, cannot impudence the coals expel
  That, for thy love, in Herod's bosom glow.
  It is as plain as water, and denial
  Makes of thy falsehood but a greater trial.   40
  Hast thou beheld thyself and could'st thou stain
  So rare perfection? Even for love of thee,
  I do profoundly hate thee. Wert thou plain,
  Thou should'st the wonder of Judea be.
  But, oh, thou art not. Hell itself lies hid   45
  Beneath thy heavenly show. Yet never wert thou chaste –
  Thou might'st exalt, pull down, command, forbid,
  And be above the wheel of fortune placed.
  Had'st thou complotted Herod's massacre

---

19   *hyssop* aromatic plant used in purification rituals.
25   *attended* endeavoured.
31   *Foul pith* The inner pith of the cedar tree rots away as the tree grows older, leaving
     its centre hollow. The meaning here is that external features do not reliably reveal
     the health of the inside.
37–8 Herod's words ironically shadow Mariam's comments about his love for Doris at
     I.ii.53–4.

That so thy son a monarch might be styled,   50
Not half so grievous such an action were
As once to think that Mariam is defiled.
Bright workmanship of nature sullied o'er
With pitchèd darkness, now thine end shall be.
Thou shalt not live, fair fiend, to cozen more   55
With heavy semblance as thou cozen'st me.
Yet must I love thee in despite of death,
And thou shalt die in the despite of love,
For neither shall my love prolong thy breath,
Nor shall thy loss of breath my love remove.   60
I might have seen thy falsehood in thy face;
Where could'st thou get thy stars that served for eyes
Except by theft, and theft is foul disgrace?
This had appeared before, were Herod wise,
But I'm a sot, a very sot, no better –   65
My wisdom long ago a'wandering fell,
Thy face, encountering it, my wit did fetter,
And made me for delight my freedom sell.
Give me my heart, false creature, 'tis a wrong
My guiltless heart should now with thine be slain.   70
Thou had'st no right to lock it up so long,
And with usurper's name I Mariam stain.

Enter BU[TLER]

HEROD
Have you designed Sohemus to his end?
BUTLER
I have, my lord.

50   Compare III.iii.75n. above.
54   *pitchèd* pitchy, black.
56   *heavy* Many editors, following Dunstan and Greg, emend to 'heav'nly'. However,
      the line makes sense as it stands: Herod believes Mariam has cozened him with
      dense, or hard-to-fathom, deceit.
67   *it* Herod's wisdom.
70   Because Herod's heart will be destroyed by his beloved Mariam's death.
71   *lock* ed. (looke Q).
72   Compare with the imagery of stained reputations earlier in the play, particularly at
      I.iv.23 and I.vi.4.
73   *designed* made over, dispatched.

HEROD   Then call our royal guard
  To do as much for Mariam.
                                                                    [*Exit* BUTLER]
                                    They offend   75
  Leave ill unblamed, or good without reward.

             [*Enter* BUTLER *with* SOLDIERS]

change mind

  Here, take her to her death. Come back, come back!
  What meant I to deprive the world of light,
  To muffle Jewry in the foulest black
  That ever was an opposite to white?   *Mariam's*
  Why, whither would you carry her?   *silence*   80
SOLDIER   You bade
  We should conduct her to her death, my lord.
HEROD
  Why, sure I did not. Herod was not mad.   *mood*
  Why should she feel the fury of the sword?   *swings*
  Oh, now the grief returns into my heart   85
  And pulls me piecemeal – love and hate do fight,
  And now hath love acquired the greater part,
  Yet now hath hate affection conquered quite.
  And, therefore, bear her hence – and, Hebrew, why
  Seize you with lion's paws the fairest lamb   90
  Of all the flock? She must not, shall not, die.
  Without her I most miserable am –
  And, with her, more than most. Away, away!
  But bear her but to prison, not to death.
           [*Exeunt* SOLDIERS *with* MARIAM]
  And is she gone, indeed? Stay, villains, stay: 95
  Her looks alone preserved your sovereign's breath.
  Well, let her go – but, yet, she shall not die:
  I cannot think she meant to poison me,
  But certain 'tis she lived too wantonly
  And, therefore, shall she never more be free   [*Exit*]   100

---

  76   *Leave* Who leave.
85–8   Herod is wracked by opposites in the manner of a Petrarchan lover.
  87   *love* ed. (boue Q).
  90   *lamb* Mariam begins, at this point, to be obliquely associated with Christ, the Lamb
      of God.
  99   *wantonly* unrestrainedly, but also with a sense of 'lasciviously'.

ACT IV, SCENE v

BUTLER

Foul villain, can thy pitchy-coloured soul
Permit thine ear to hear her causeless doom
And not enforce thy tongue that tale control
That must unjustly bring her to her tomb?
Oh, Salome, thou hast thyself repaid   5
For all the benefits that thou hast done,
Thou art the cause I have the queen betrayed,
Thou hast my heart to darkest falsehood won.
I am condemned: heav'n gave me not my tongue
To slander innocents, to lie, deceive,   10
To be the hateful instrument to wrong,
The earth of greatest glory to bereave.
My sin ascends and doth to heaven cry
It is the blackest deed that ever was,
And there doth sit an angel notary   15
That doth record it down in leaves of brass.
Oh, how my heart doth quake. Achitophel,
Thou found'st a means thyself from shame to free,
And sure my soul approves thou did'st not well –
All follow some, and I will follow thee.   [*Exit*]   20

[handwritten margin notes: "blame on Salome", "heavenly justice"]

0   s.d. ed. (Actus 4. Scoena 5. Q).
1   *pitchy-coloured* Compare IV.iv.54. The verbal repetition draws a parallel between
      Herod's unjust accusation of Mariam and the Butler's justified accusation of
      himself, underlining the impossibility of judging a person's inside by their
      appearance.
2   *causeless* ed. (caules Q).
3   *control* rebuke.
13–14 Certain sins, including wilful murder, are said to cry out to heaven for retribution
      (see, for example, Genesis 4.10). The Butler believes he is wilfully complicit in
      Mariam's death.
15   *notary* secretary, clerk.
15–16 On Judgement Day, the dead will be judged according to their works as written
      down in the books of life (see Revelation 20.12). Brass tablets were used for
      permanent inscriptions (see 1 Maccabees 14.27).
17   *Achitophel* King David's counsellor, who defected to Absalom and hanged himself
      when his counsel was unheeded (see 2 Samuel 15–17).
19   *approves* attests. The Butler is either saying that Achitophel's actions were wrong
      and he was therefore right to kill himself; or that his suicide was wrong, but that he
      (the Butler) will follow his example.

ACT IV, SCENE vi

[*Enter*] CONSTABARUS, BABA'S SONS, *and their* GUARD

CONSTABARUS
    Now here we step our last, the way to death;
    We must not tread this way a second time.
    Yet let us resolutely yield our breath;
    Death is the only ladder, heaven to climb.

FIRST SON
    With willing mind I could myself resign,   5
    But yet it grieves me with a grief untold,
    Our death should be accompanied with thine;
    Our friendship we to thee have dearly sold.

CONSTABARUS
    Still wilt thou wrong the sacred name of friend?
    Then should'st thou never style it friendship more,   10
    But base mechanic traffic that doth lend,
    Yet will be sure they shall the debt restore.
    I could, with needless complement, return:
    'Tis for thy ceremony, I could say;
    'Tis I that made the fire your house to burn,   15
    For but for me, she would not you betray.
    Had not the damnèd woman sought mine end
    You had not been the subject of her hate;
    You never did her hateful mind offend,
    Nor could your deaths have freed her nuptial fate.   20
    Therefore, fair friends, though you were still unborn,
    Some other subtlety devised should be

---

  0   s.d. ed. (Actus 4. Scoena 6. Q).
  8   *we . . . sold* has cost you dearly.
  9   Compare II.ii.13–14.
10   *style* call.
11   *mechanic traffic* vulgar trade.
12   *they* those to whom commodities are lent.
13   *complement* addition. Weller and Ferguson emend to 'compliment' but this seems
      unnecessary.
      return reply.
14   i.e. It is to requite your politeness that I could say. (Weller and Ferguson emend
      ''Tis' to 'This', while Dunstan and Greg suggest emending to 'Thus'. However, the
      line makes some sense as it stands.)
20   *her* ed. (your Q).

Whereby my life, though guiltless, should be torn.
Thus have I proved: 'tis you that die for me.
And, therefore, should I weakly now lament,   25
You have but done your duties – friends should die
Alone their friends' disaster to prevent,
Though not compelled by strong necessity.
But now farewell, fair city, never more
Shall I behold your beauty shining bright;   30
Farewell of Jewish men the worthy store,
But no farewell to any <u>female wight</u>.
You wavering crew, my curse to you I leave.
You had but one to give you any grace,
And you, yourselves, will Mariam's life bereave.   35
Your commonwealth doth innocency chase;
You creatures made to be the human curse,
You tigers, lionesses, hungry bears,
Tear-massacring hyenas – nay, far worse –
For they for prey do shed their feignèd tears,   40
But you will weep (you creatures cross to good)
For your unquenchèd thirst of human blood.
You were the angels cast from heaven for pride,
And still do keep your angels' outward show,
But none of you are inly beautified,   45
For still your heaven-depriving pride doth grow.
Did not the sins of many require a scourge,

[handwritten marginal note: hates women]

25–8   i.e. And, therefore, even though I might lament a little, you have only done your
       duties (by dying for me): friends should die solely to prevent their friends' disaster,
       even though they are not compelled to do so.
26–7   *friends . . . prevent* See John 15.13: 'Greater love than this hath no man, when any
       man bestoweth his life for his friends'.
31   *store* group, number.
32   *wight* person.
36   *chase* drive out.
37   *human curse* because Eve initiated mankind's fall (see Genesis 3).
41   *cross* contrary, opposed.
43   Religious tradition suggested that rebel angels were cast out of heaven, becoming
       demons under the command of Satan. The story is developed from biblical
       passages including Isaiah 14.12–15 and Revelation 12.7–9.
44–6   Constabarus adds his voice to the discussion of insides and outsides: compare, for
       example, IV.iv.17–20, 31–4.
47   *scourge* whip.

Your place on earth had been by this withstood,
But since a flood no more the world must purge,
You stayed in office of a second flood.   50
You giddy creatures, sowers of debate,
You'll love today and for no other cause
But for you, yesterday, did deeply hate.
You are the wreck of order, breach of laws.
You, best, are foolish, froward, wanton, vain;   55
Your worst, adulterous, murderous, cunning, proud:
And Salome attends the latter train,
Or, rather, she their leader is allowed.
I do the sottishness of men bewail
That do with following you enhance your pride.   60
'Twere better that the human race should fail
Than be by such a mischief multiplied.
Cham's servile curse to all your sex was given
Because in paradise you did offend.
Then do we not resist the will of heaven   65
When on your wills, like servants, we attend?
You are to nothing constant but to ill;
You are with nought but wickedness endued;
Your loves are set on nothing but your will,
And thus my censure I of you conclude –   70
You are the least of goods, the worst of evils;
Your best are worse than men, your worst than devils.

---

48   *this* women's pride.
     withstood opposed. Women's continued existence on earth would have been
     opposed or challenged if it were not that people's sins were chastised by their
     presence.
50   *in office* in the place of.
51   *debate* dissention.
55   *You . . . are* At best you are. (Weller and Ferguson emend to 'Your' to balance with
     l. 56.)
     froward perverse. Compare IV.iii.53n. above.
57   *attends . . . train* is associated with the second group (of adulterers, murderers, etc.).
58   *she* ed. (he Q).
59   *sottishness* foolishness.
63   See Genesis 9.20–7 where the descendants of Ham (or Cham), son of Noah, are
     cursed with eternal servitude because Ham revealed his father's sleeping nakedness
     to his brothers. Constabarus extends this curse to all women because of Eve's part
     in the fall of mankind.
68   *endued* endowed.
70   *censure* condemnation.

SECOND SON

    Come let us to our death. Are we not blessed?
    Our death will freedom from these creatures give,
    Those trouble-quiet sowers of unrest.   75
    And this I vow that, had I leave to live,
    I would forever lead a single life
    And never venture on a devilish wife.

                                   [*Exeunt*]

ACT IV, SCENE vii

[*Enter*] HEROD *and* SALOME

HEROD

    Nay, she shall die. Die, quoth you? That she shall –
    But for the means? The means! Methinks 'tis hard
    To find a means to murder her withal,
    Therefore I am resolved she shall be spared.

SALOME

    Why? Let her be beheaded.

HEROD   That were well.   5

    Think you that swords are miracles like you?
    Her skin will every curtl'ax edge refel,
    And then your enterprise you well may rue.
    What if the fierce Arabian notice take
    Of this your wretched weaponless estate?   10
    They answer, when we bid resistance make,

---

76   *leave* permission.

0   s.d. ed. (Actus 4. Scoena 7. Q).

1   Herod, now in the company of Salome, appears to be continuing his train of
    thought from IV.iv.97 above.

6   *miracles* of hardness, cruelty: see ll. 35–6 below.

7   *curtl'ax* cutlass, sword.
    refel repulse.

8   *rue* regret.

9   *fierce Arabian* possibly Silleus, but probably, more generally, the Arabians with
    whom Herod had recently been at war: see II.iv.58 and note above.

10   *your* possibly a compositor's error for 'our'.

11   i.e. Jerusalem's people reply, when we ask them to fight (against the Arabians).

That Mariam's skin their falchions did rebate.
Beware of this. You make a goodly hand
If you of weapons do deprive our land.

SALOME
Why drown her then.

HEROD   Indeed, a sweet device.   15
Why, would not every river turn her course
Rather than do her beauty prejudice,
And be reverted to the proper source
So not a drop of water should be found
In all Judea's quondam fertile ground?   20

SALOME
Then let the fire devour her.

HEROD   'Twill not be.
Flame is from her derived into my heart.
Thou nursest flame; flame will not murder thee,
My fairest Mariam, fullest of desert.

SALOME
Then let her live for me.

HEROD   Nay, she shall die.   25
But can you live without her?

SALOME   Doubt you that?

HEROD
I'm sure I cannot. I beseech you try.
I have experience, but I know not what.

SALOME
How should I try?

HEROD   Why, let my love be slain,
But if we cannot live without her sight,   30
You'll find the means to make her breathe again,
Or else you will bereave my comfort quite.

SALOME
Oh, ay. I warrant you.   [Exit]

---

12 *falchions ... rebate* blunted their broadswords.
13 *hand* case, position.
17 *prejudice* harm.
18 *reverted* turned back.
    proper original.
20 *quondam* formerly.
22 *derived* conveyed.
24 *desert* excellence (with a faint, contradictory echo, following ll. 19–20, of desert as barren wilderness).

HEROD   What, is she gone,
   And gone to bid the world be overthrown?
   What, is her heart's composure hardest stone?   35
   To what a pass are cruel women grown?

             [*Enter* SALOME]

   She is returned already. Have you done?
   Is't possible you can command so soon
   A creature's heart to quench the flaming sun,
   Or from the sky to wipe away the moon?   40
SALOME
   If Mariam be the sun and moon, it is,
   For I already have commanded this.
HEROD
   But have you seen her cheek?
SALOME   A thousand times.
HEROD
   But did you mark it, too?
SALOME   Ay, very well.
HEROD
   What is't?
SALOME   A crimson bush that ever limes   45
   The soul whose foresight doth not much excel.
HEROD
   Send word she shall not die. Her cheek a bush?
   Nay, then I see indeed you marked it not.
SALOME
   'Tis very fair, but yet will never blush
   Though foul dishonours do her forehead blot.   50
HEROD
   Then let her die. 'Tis very true indeed,
   And for this fault alone shall Mariam bleed.

---

  44   *mark* pay proper attention to.
45–6 Purkiss says the comparison of Mariam's cheek to a bush spread with sticky lime
     to catch birds 'is awkward, to say the least'. However, there might also be a
     blasphemous reference to the burning bush of Exodus 3: Salome likens Mariam's
     entrapment of unwary souls to the bush that intrigued Moses and prefigured his
     reception of the Ten Commandments, several of which Salome is in the process of
     breaking.
49–50 Compare Constabarus's accusation of Salome at I.vi.3–4 and Salome's description
     of herself at I.iv.23–32.

SALOME

    What fault, my lord?

HEROD   What fault is't? You that ask,

    If you be ignorant, I know of none.

    To call her back from death shall be your task.   55

    I'm glad that she for innocent is known,

    For on the brow of Mariam hangs a fleece,

    Whose slenderest twine is strong enough to bind

    The hearts of kings. The pride and shame of Greece,

    Troy-flaming Helen's, not so fairly shined.   60

SALOME

    'Tis true indeed. She lays them out for nets

    To catch the hearts that do not shun a bait.

    'Tis time to speak, for Herod sure forgets

    That Mariam's very tresses hide deceit.

HEROD

    Oh, do they so? Nay, then, you do but well.   65

    In sooth, I thought it had been hair.

    Nets, call you them? Lord, how they do excel –

    I never saw a net that showed so fair.

    But have you heard her speak?

SALOME   You know I have.

HEROD

    And were you not amazed?

SALOME   No, not a whit.   70

HEROD

    Then 'twas not her you heard – her life I'll save,

    For Mariam hath a world-amazing wit.

SALOME

    She speaks a beauteous language, but within

    Her heart is false as powder and her tongue

---

57   *fleece* A reference to the golden fleece sought and won by Jason and the Argonauts.
     This comparison was common in contemporary love poetry.

60   *Troy-flaming Helen* The abduction of the Grecian Helen by the Trojan Paris caused
     the war that destroyed Troy. Helen's name was synonymous with lasciviousness.

61   *them* her tresses (l. 64 below).

72   *world-amazing wit* Herod, like Pheroras, is attracted by his wife's intelligence: see
     III.i.23–8. As with Pheroras, Salome attempts to undermine this attraction.

74   *false as powder* A reference either to gunpowder, used to undermine buildings, or
     to cosmetic powder, which deceptively colours the face (see Introduction). In both
     cases, Salome participates in the play's obsession with insides and outsides.

Doth but allure the auditors to sin 75
And is the instrument to do you wrong.

HEROD

It may be so. Nay, 'tis so. She's unchaste:
Her mouth will ope to every stranger's ear.
Then let the executioner make haste
Lest she enchant him if her words he hear. 80
Let him be deaf, lest she do him surprise,
That shall to free her spirit be assigned.
Yet what boots deafness if he have his eyes?
Her murderer must be both deaf and blind,
For if he see, he needs must see the stars 85
That shine on either side of Mariam's face,
Whose sweet aspect will terminate the wars
Wherewith he should a soul so precious chase.
Her eyes can speak and, in their speaking, move.
Oft did my heart with reverence receive 90
The world's mandates. Pretty tales of love
They utter, which can human bondage weave.
But shall I let this heaven's model die
Which, for a small self-portraiture, she drew?
Her eyes like stars, her forehead like the sky – 95
She is like heaven and must be heavenly true.

SALOME

Your thoughts do rave with doting on the queen.
Her eyes are ebon hewed and, you'll confess,
A sable star hath been but seldom seen.
Then speak of reason more, of Mariam less. 100

HEROD

Yourself are held a goodly creature here,
Yet so unlike my Mariam in your shape
That, when to her you have approachèd near,

---

75 *auditors* listeners.
78 *ope* open (*OED*, ope, *v*.). Compare I.vi.3 and III.iii.65.
83 *boots* avails.
88 *chase* drive (from its body).
89 *move* disturb others emotionally.
91 *mandates* commands.
94 *she* heaven: i.e. heaven made Mariam in her likeness.
95 *Her* Mariam.
98 *ebon hewed* coloured black as ebony.

Myself hath often ta'en you for an ape.

And yet you prate of beauty. Go your ways.   105

You are to her a sunburnt blackamoor,

Your paintings cannot equal Mariam's praise,

Her nature is so rich, you are so poor.

Let her be stayed from death for, if she die,

We do we know not what to stop her breath.   110

A world cannot another Mariam buy.

Why stay you ling'ring? Countermand her death.

SALOME

Then you'll no more remember what hath past –

Sohemus' love and hers shall be forgot.

'Tis well, in truth. That fault may be her last   115

And she may mend, though yet she love you not.

HEROD

Oh, God! 'Tis true. Sohemus! Earth and heaven,

Why did you both conspire to make me cursed

In cozening me with shows and proofs uneven?

She showed the best and yet did prove the worst.   120

Her show was such as had our singing king,

The holy David, Mariam's beauty seen,

The Hittites had then felt no deadly sting,

Nor Bethsabe had never been a queen.

Or had his son, the wisest man of men,   125

Whose fond delight did most consist in change,

Beheld her face, he had been stayed again –

105 *prate* A derogatory choice of verb to describe Salome's speech: compare with 'whine' at IV.ii.35 above.

106 *sunburnt blackamoor* This image might have contemporary resonance with Queen Anna's performance as an Ethiopian in *The Masque of Blackness* (1605). See also Dympna Callaghan on issues of race in *Mariam* ('Re-reading Elizabeth Cary's *The Tragedie of Mariam, Faire Queene of Jewry*', *Women, 'Race,' and Writing in the Early Modern Period*, ed. Margo Hendricks and Patricia Parker (1994), pp. 163–77).

107 *paintings* face paintings with cosmetics.

110 Weller and Ferguson see an echo here of Luke 23.34: 'They know not what they do'. Mariam is increasingly associated with Christ as the play progresses.

119 *cozening* defrauding.

  uneven i.e. the appearance and the reality of things did not match.

121–4 See 2 Samuel 11 in which David conceives a child with Bathsheba (Bethsabe), wife of Uriah, the Hittite, and arranges for her husband's death in battle.

125–7 See 1 Kings 11 which describes how Solomon, son of David and Bathsheba, loved many women.

127 *stayed* halted, restrained.

No creature, having her, can wish to range.
Had Asuerus seen my Mariam's brow,
The humble Jew, she might have walked alone.   130
Her beauteous virtue should have stayed below
Whiles Mariam mounted to the Persian throne.
But what avails it all for in the weight
She is deceitful, light as vanity.
Oh, she was made for nothing but a bait   *object*   135
To train some hapless man to misery.
I am the hapless man that have been trained
To endless bondage. I will see her yet.
Methinks I should discern her if she feigned –
Can human eyes be dazed by woman's wit?   140
Once more these eyes of mine with hers shall meet
Before the headsman do her life bereave.
Shall I forever part from thee, my sweet,
Without the taking of my latest leave?

SALOME

You had as good resolve to save her now.   145
I'll stay her death. 'Tis well determinèd,
For sure she never more will break her vow –
Sohemus and Josephus both are dead.

HEROD

She shall not live, nor will I see her face;
A long-healed wound a second time doth bleed.   150
With Joseph I remember her disgrace –
A shameful end ensues a shameful deed.
Oh, that I had not called to mind anew
The discontent of Mariam's wavering heart.
'Twas you, you foul-mouthed Ate, none but you,   155
That did the thought hereof to me impart.
Hence from my sight, my black tormenter, hence,

129–30   See Esther 2 in which Ahasuerus, king of Persia, marries Esther, Cary's 'humble
         Jew'.
133   *weight* scales.
136   *train* drag.
         hapless unlucky.
139   *feigned* dissembled.
146   *stay* stop, prevent.
         determinèd concluded.
152   *ensues* results from.
155   *Ate* Greek goddess of discord, delusion and recklessness.

For had'st not thou made Herod unsecure,
I had not doubted Mariam's innocence,
But still had held her in my heart for pure.   160

SALOME

I'll leave you to your passion. 'Tis no time
To purge me now, though of a guiltless crime.   *Exit*

HEROD

Destruction take thee; thou hast made my heart
As heavy as revenge. I am so dull,
Methinks I am not sensible of smart,   165
Though hideous horrors at my bosom pull.
My head weighs downwards, therefore will I go
To try if I can sleep away my woe.   [*Exit*]

ACT IV, SCENE viii

[*Enter* MARIAM]

MARIAM

Am I the Mariam that presumed so much
And deemed my face must needs preserve my breath?
Ay, I it was that thought my beauty such
As it alone could countermand my death.
Now death will teach me; he can pale as well   5
A cheek of roses as a cheek less bright,
And dim an eye whose shine doth most excel
As soon as one that casts a meaner light.
Had not myself against myself conspired,
No plot, no adversary from without,   10
Could Herod's love from Mariam have retired,
Or from his heart have thrust my semblance out.
The wanton queen that never loved for love,

---

162   *purge me* exonerate myself.
165   *sensible of smart* sensitive to pain.

  0   s.d. ed. (Actus 4. Scoena. 8. Q).
  4   *As* ed. (At Q).
 11   *retired* withdrawn.

False Cleopatra, wholly set on gain,
With all her slights did prove, yet vainly prove,   15
For her the love of Herod to obtain.
Yet her allurements, all her courtly guile,
Her smiles, her favours, and her smooth deceit,
Could not my face from Herod's mind exile,
But were with him of less than little weight.   20
That face and person that in Asia late
For beauty's goddess, Paphos' queen, was ta'en,
That face that did captive great Julius' fate,
That very face that was Antonius' bane,
That face that to be Egypt's pride was born,   25
That face that all the world esteemed so rare,
Did Herod hate, despise, neglect, and scorn,
When with the same he Mariam's did compare.
This made that I improvidently wrought,
And on the wager even my life did pawn,   30
Because I thought, and yet but truly thought,
That Herod's love could not from me be drawn.
But now, though out of time, I plainly see
It could be drawn, though never drawn from me.
Had I but with humility been graced,   35
As well as fair, I might have proved me wise,
But I did think, because I knew me chaste,
One virtue for a woman might suffice;
That mind for glory of our sex might stand
Wherein humility and chastity   40
Doth march with equal paces hand in hand,
But one, if single seen, who setteth by?
And I had singly one, but 'tis my joy
That I was ever innocent, though sour,

15   *prove* attempt.
22   *Paphos' queen* Venus, whose temple was at Paphos in Cyprus.
     ta'en mistaken.
23   *captive* hold captive, captivate.
     Julius Julius Caesar.
24   *Antonius* Mark Antony.
     bane ruin.
38   *One virtue* Her chastity.
42   i.e. Who cares if only one virtue (either humility or chastity) is perceived (in a
     woman's mind).

85

And therefore can they but my life destroy –   45
My soul is free from adversaries' power.

Enter DORIS

You princes, great in power and high in birth,
Be great and high. I envy not your hap.
Your birth must be from dust, your power on earth;
In heaven shall Mariam sit in Sarah's lap.   50

DORIS

Ay, heaven! Your beauty cannot bring you thither.
Your soul is black and spotted, full of sin;
You in adult'ry lived nine year together,
And heaven will never let adult'ry in.

MARIAM

What art thou, that dost poor Mariam pursue –   55
Some spirit sent to drive me to despair?
Who sees for truth that Mariam is untrue?
If fair she be, she is as chaste as fair.

DORIS

I am that Doris that was once beloved,
Beloved by Herod, Herod's lawful wife.   60
'Twas you that Doris from his side removed,
And robbed from me the glory of my life.

MARIAM

Was that adult'ry? Did not Moses say
That he that, being matched, did deadly hate,
Might by permission put his wife away   65
And take a more beloved to be his mate?

DORIS

What did he hate me for? For simple truth?
For bringing beauteous babes, for love to him,
For riches, noble birth, or tender youth,

---

46   *adversaries* enemies, but, as Weller and Ferguson point out, this term carried
     specific theological overtones and also referred to Satan.
48   *hap* fortune.
50   *Sarah's lap* Sarah was the wife of Abraham (Genesis 16–21). The phrase is
     analogous to the bosom of Abram mentioned above at I.ii.9–10.
63–6 *Moses . . . mate* See Deuteronomy 24.1–5.
68   *bringing* giving birth to.

Or for no stain did Doris honour dim?   70
Oh, tell me, Mariam, tell me, if you know,
Which fault of these made Herod Doris' foe.
These thrice three years have I, with hands held up
And bowèd knees, fast nailèd to the ground,
Besought for thee the dregs of that same cup,   75
That cup of wrath that is for sinners found. *Sad*
And now thou art to drink it. Doris' curse
Upon thyself did all this while attend,
But now it shall pursue thy children worse.

MARIAM   *children*

Oh, Doris, now to thee my knees I bend,   80
That heart that never bowed, to thee doth bow.
Curse not mine infants – let it thee suffice
That heaven doth punishment to me allow.
Thy curse is cause that guiltless Mariam dies.

DORIS

Had I ten thousand tongues and every tongue   85
Inflamed with poison's power and steeped in gall,
My curses would not answer for my wrong,
Though I, in cursing thee, employed them all.
Hear thou, that did'st Mount Gerizim command
To be a place whereon with cause to curse: 90
Stretch thy revenging arm, thrust forth thy hand,
And plague the mother much, the children worse.
Throw flaming fire upon the baseborn heads
That were begotten in unlawful beds,   *how to*
But let them live till they have sense to know   *for*   95
What 'tis to be in miserable state.   *reverse*
Then be their nearest friends their overthrow,
Attended be they by suspicious hate,

---

70   *for* because.
76   *cup of wrath* See, for example, Jeremiah 25.15–38 and Ezekiel 23.31–4.
78   *attend* accompany you.
89   *Gerizim* ed. (*Gerarim* Q). In Deuteronomy 27, Moses commands some of the
      Israelites to stand on Mount Gerizim and bless the people, and some to stand on
      the neighbouring Mount Ebal and curse. Cary seems to have confused the two
      mountains.
91   This echoes Ezekiel 25.16: 'Therefore thus saith ye Lord God; Behold, I will stretch
      out mine hand upon the Philistines'.

And, Mariam, I do hope this boy of mine
Shall one day come to be the death of thine.   *Exit*   100

MARIAM

Oh, heaven forbid! I hope the world shall see
This curse of thine shall be returned on thee.
Now, earth, farewell, though I be yet but young,
Yet I, methinks, have known thee too, too long.   *Exit*

[CHORUS]

CHORUS

The fairest action of our human life   105
Is scorning to revenge an injury,
For who forgives without a further strife
His adversary's heart to him doth tie,
    And 'tis a firmer conquest, truly said,
    To win the heart than overthrow the head.   110

If we a worthy enemy do find
To yield to worth, it must be nobly done,
But if of baser metal be his mind,
In base revenge there is no honour won.
    Who would a worthy courage overthrow   115
    And who would wrestle with a worthless foe?

We say our hearts are great and cannot yield;
Because they cannot yield, it proves them poor.
Great hearts are tasked beyond their power, but seld
The weakest lion will the loudest roar.   120

99–100   *this ... thine* Doris's curse was fruitful: her son, Antipater, was instrumental in the downfall of Mariam's children, Alexander and Aristobolus: see *Ant.*, 16.7.417–16.17.435.

105–10   The Chorus's sentiments might be inspired by the first chapter of Montaigne's *Essays*, 'By diverse means men come unto a like end'. Their ideas about revenge seem anachronistic to the play's historical period as they chime strongly with New Testament teaching (see, for example, Luke 6.35 or Matthew 5.38–41). However, revenge is forbidden in Leviticus 19.18, and the Proverbs advocate kindness towards one's enemies (Proverbs 24.17, 25.21–2).

111–12   i.e. It is noble to yield to a worthy enemy.

113   *metal* material, with a pun on 'mettle', meaning 'disposition'.

117–22   The stanza presents the paradox that sometimes the only way to be great is to yield.

119   *tasked* assigned work, burdened.
      seld seldom (i.e. not often, sometimes).

119–20   Moving the comma to the end of line 119 renders the meaning: 'Great hearts are

Truth's school for certain doth this same allow:
High heartedness doth sometimes teach to bow.

A noble heart doth teach a virtuous scorn:
To scorn to owe a duty over-long,
To scorn to be for benefits forborne,   125
To scorn to lie, to scorn to do a wrong,
    To scorn to bear an injury in mind,
    To scorn a free-born heart, slave-like, to bind.

But if for wrongs we needs revenge must have,
Then be our vengeance of the noblest kind.   130
Do we his body from our fury save
And let our hate prevail against our mind?
    What can 'gainst him a greater vengeance be
    Than make his foe more worthy far than he?

[handwritten marginal note: moralizing on revenge]

Had Mariam scorned to leave a due unpaid,   135
She would to Herod then have paid her love,
And not have been by sullen passion swayed.
To fix her thoughts all injury above
    Is virtuous pride. Had Mariam thus been proved,
    Long famous life to her had been allowed.   140

seldom burdened beyond their capabilities'. Retaining Q's comma after 'power'
supports the sense of line 122, rendering the meaning: 'Great hearts are burdened
beyond their capabilities, but sometimes the weakest lion will roar loudest' (i.e.
sometimes to yield is to be strong).

124   *duty* obligation.
125   i.e. To scorn to be treated leniently from gratitude for former kindnesses (Weller
     and Ferguson).
131–2 i.e. Should we turn our hatred against ourselves rather than commit violence upon
     the bodies of our enemies?
133–4 i.e. What can be a greater revenge against a foe than making ourselves more virtu-
     ous than him (because we have turned the other cheek). The sentiment is strongly
     Christian and was expounded in Protestant and Catholic catechisms under the
     commandment, 'Thou shalt not kill'.
135   *scorned . . . unpaid* disdained to leave a debt unpaid (i.e. decided that she must pay
     her debt).
139   *proved* tested.

ACT V, SCENE i

[*Enter* NUNTIO]

NUNTIO

    When, sweetest friend, did I so far offend
    Your heavenly self, that you, my fault to quit,
    Have made me now relater of her end –
    The end of beauty, chastity and wit?
    Was none so hapless in the fatal place,   5
    But I, most wretched, for the queen t'choose?
    'Tis certain I have some ill-boding face
    That made me culled to tell this luckless news.
    And yet no news to Herod. Were it new
    To him, unhappy t'had not been at all –   10
    Yet do I long to come within his view
    That he may know his wife did guiltless fall.

[*Enter* HEROD]

    And here he comes. [*To* HEROD] Your Mariam greets you well.

HEROD

    What? Lives my Mariam? Joy, exceeding joy.
    She shall not die.

NUNTIO   Heaven doth your will repel.   15

HEROD

    Oh, do not with thy words my life destroy.

---

    0   s.d. ed. (Actus quintus. Scoena prima. Q).
    1   *sweetest friend* Weller and Ferguson gloss as 'Mariam', but it is possible, particularly
        in light of 'her' in l. 3, that the Nuntio is addressing a divinity.
    2   *quit* repay, requite.
    3   *her* Weller and Ferguson emend to 'your', but the Nuntio goes on to refer to
        Mariam in the third person in l. 6, so 'her' makes sense as it stands.
    5   *hapless* unlucky.
        fatal place place of execution.
    6   *queen* i.e. Mariam.
    8   *culled* selected.
 9–10   The implication is that, had Mariam's execution been news to Herod, he would
        have prevented it.
   12   s.d. in Q is after l. 13.
   15   *repel* force back.

I prithee, tell no dying-tale. Thine eye,
Without thy tongue, doth tell but too, too much.
Yet let thy tongue's addition make me die:
Death welcome comes to him whose grief is such.   20

NUNTIO

I went amongst the curious gazing troop
To see the last of her that was the best,
To see if death had heart to make her stoop,
To see the sun-admiring Phoenix nest.
When there I came, upon the way I saw   25
The stately Mariam, not debased by fear.
Her look did seem to keep the world in awe,
Yet mildly did her face this fortune bear.

HEROD

Thou dost usurp my right. My tongue was framed, *meta*
To be the instrument of Mariam's praise.   30
Yet, speak. She cannot be too often famed;
All tongues suffice not her sweet name to raise.

NUNTIO

But as she came, she Alexandra met,
Who did her death – sweet queen – no whit bewail,
But as if nature she did quite forget,   35
She did upon her daughter loudly rail.

HEROD

Why stopped you not her mouth? Where had she words
To darken that that heaven made so bright?
Our sacred tongue no epithet affords
To call her other than the world's delight.   40

NUNTIO

She told her that her death was too, too good,
And that already she had lived too long.

---

21   *curious . . . troop* This moment echoes Christ's passion: see Matthew 27.47–56 and
     Luke 23.27–35.
24   *sun-admiring Phoenix* The mythical Phoenix periodically regenerated itself out of
     the flames of its nest. It was adopted in Christian symbolism as a sign of Christ and
     the resurrection.
27   *keep . . . awe* An oblique echo of Psalm 33.8.
36   Compare *Ant.*, 15.11.399 where Alexandra scolds her daughter 'injuriously'. It is
     also possible that this moment echoes Peter's denial of Jesus: see, for example, Luke
     22.54–62.
38   *darken* ed. (darke Q). Emended to regularise the metre.

She said she shamed to have a part in blood
Of her that did the princely Herod wrong.

HEROD

Base, pickthank devil. Shame? 'Twas all her glory   45
That she to noble Mariam was the mother,
But never shall it live in any story –
Her name, except to infamy, I'll smother.
What answer did her princely daughter make?

NUNTIO

She made no answer, but she looked the while   50
As if thereof she scarce did notice take,
Yet smiled a dutiful, though scornful, smile.

HEROD

Sweet creature, I that look to mind do call –
Full oft hath Herod been amazed withal.
Go on.

NUNTIO   She came unmoved with pleasant grace,   55
As if to triumph her arrival were,
In stately habit and with cheerful face,
Yet ev'ry eye was moist, but Mariam's there.
When justly opposite to me she came,
She picked me out from all the crew,   60
She beckoned to me, called me by my name,
For she my name, my birth, and fortune knew.

HEROD

What? Did she name thee? Happy, happy man.
Wilt thou not ever love that name the better?
But what sweet tune did this fair dying swan   65
Afford thine ear? Tell all, omit no letter.

NUNTIO

'Tell thou my lord', said she . . .

HEROD   Me, meant she me?
Is't true? The more my shame. I was her lord.

43   *to . . . blood* to be related to.
45   *pickthank* sycophant.
52   Compare Mariam's forbearing response to her mother in *Ant.*, 15.11.399.
55   *Go on* ed. (*Nun.* Go on Q). Although 'Go on' is given to the Nuntio in Q, it makes
     more sense as Herod's speech.
56   *triumph* i.e. a Roman triumphal procession.
59   *justly* exactly.
60   *crew* company, crowd.
65   *sweet . . . swan* The mute swan is said to sing only once – as it dies.

92

Were I not mad, her lord I still should be,
But now her name must be by me adored.   70
Oh, say, what said she more? Each word she said
Shall be the food whereon my heart is fed.

NUNTIO

'Tell thou my lord, thou saw'st me lose my breath.'

HEROD

Oh, that I could that sentence now control.

NUNTIO

'If guiltily eternal be my death . . .'   75

HEROD

I hold her chaste even in my inmost soul.   *doesn't understand*

NUNTIO

'By three days hence, if wishes could revive,
I know himself would make me oft alive.'

HEROD

Three days? Three hours, three minutes – not so much –
A minute in a thousand parts divided.   80
My penitency for her death is such
As, in the first, I wished she had not died.
But forward in thy tale.

NUNTIO   Why, on she went
And after she some silent prayer had said,
She did as if to die she were content,   85
And thus to heaven her heavenly soul is fled.

HEROD

But art thou sure there doth no life remain?

---

69 *mad, her lord* ed. (made her lord, Q). Weller and Ferguson suggest the emendation
    followed here. Purkiss glosses Q's original spelling and punctuation as: 'Had I not
    been her king, I would still be her husband'.

73 *lose* ed. (loose Q). Weller and Ferguson suggest Q's original spelling accords greater
    agency to Mariam who is in control of loosing (i.e. letting out) her breath in
    speech.

74 *sentence* understood both as a legal sentence and a linguistic one.
    control hinder, prevent.

75 i.e. If I am judged guilty after my death and spend eternity in hell.

77 *three days* an allusion to the time spent by Christ in the tomb: see Luke 24.7.

82 *in the first* in the first of the divided minutes. Compare Herod's evocation of time
    at IV.i.17–20.

85 *did* made, although this could be modernised to 'died': see l. 190 below where 'did'
    more clearly means 'died'.

Is't possible my Mariam should be dead?
Is there no trick to make her breathe again?

NUNTIO

Her body is divided from her head.] *comme*   90

HEROD

Why yet methinks there might be found, by art,
Strange ways of cure. 'Tis sure, rare things are done
By an inventive head and willing heart.

NUNTIO

Let not, my lord, your fancies idly run.
It is as possible, it should be seen,   95
That we should make the holy Abraham live,
Though he entombed two thousand years had been,
As breath again to slaughtered Mariam give.
But now, for more assaults prepare your ears.

HEROD

There cannot be a further cause of moan;   100
This accident shall shelter me from fears.
What can I fear? Already Mariam's gone.
Yet tell e'en what you will.

NUNTIO   As I came by
From Mariam's death, I saw upon a tree
A man that to his neck a cord did tie,   105
Which cord he had designed his end to be.
When me he once discerned, he downwards bowed,
And thus with fearful voice he cried aloud:
Go tell the king he trusted ere he tried.
I am the cause that Mariam causeless died. / *suicide of*   110
                                                    the butler

HEROD

Damnation take him, for it was the slave
That said she meant, with poison's deadly force,
To end my life that she the crown might have –

---

91 *art* specifically magical or alchemical art.
92 *rare* unusual, strange.
96–7 *holy. . . years* According to biblical chronology, Abraham had been dead for two
       thousand years at the time the play was set. For Abraham, see I.ii.9–10n.
105–6 *man . . . be* This episode echoes the biblical story of Judas, the betrayer of Christ
       (see Matthew 27.3–5). It is original to Cary's play, and not found in Josephus.
108 *he* ed. (she Q).
109 Compare the Chorus's words at II.iv.122.

Which tale did Mariam from herself divorce.
Oh, pardon me, thou pure, unspotted ghost. 115
My punishment must needs sufficient be
In missing that content I valued most,
Which was thy admirable face to see.
I had but one inestimable jewel,
Yet one I had, no monarch had the like, 120
And therefore may I curse myself as cruel.
'Twas broken by a blow myself did strike.
I gazed thereon and never thought me blessed,
But when on it my dazzled eye might rest.
A precious mirror made by wondrous art, 125
I prized it ten times dearer than my crown
And laid it up fast folded in my heart,
Yet I, in sudden choler, cast it down
And pashed it all to pieces. 'Twas no foe
That robbed me of it; no Arabian host, 130
Nor no Armenian guide hath used me so,
But Herod's wretched self hath Herod crossed.
She was my graceful moiety; me, accurst,
To slay my better half and save my worst.
But sure she is not dead. You did but jest *cannot* 135
To put me in perplexity a while. *behue*
'Twere well, indeed, if I could so be dressed.
I see she is alive; methinks you smile.

NUNTIO

If sainted Abel yet deceased be,
'Tis certain Mariam is as dead as he. 140

HEROD

Why, then go call her to me; bid her now
Put on fair habit, stately ornament,

---

114 Mariam denied (or distanced herself from) the story (that she had meant to poison
Herod).
117 *content* contentment.
128 *choler* anger: see I.iii.22n.
129 *pashed* smashed.
130–1 *Arabian host ... Armenian guide* For Herod's Arabian wars, see *Ant.*, 15.6.390ff. For
Mark Antony's wars in Armenia at around the same time, see *Ant.*, 15.5.389.
133 *moiety* half: compare IV.iii.2.
137 *dressed* directed, i.e. set up, tricked.
139 *sainted Abel* See Genesis 4.2–8. Slain by his brother Cain, Abel was seen as a
prefiguration of Christ.

And let no frown o'ershade her smoothest brow:
In her doth Herod place his whole content.

NUNTIO

She'll come in stately weeds to please your sense,   145
If now she come attired in robe of heaven.
Remember you yourself did send her hence,
And now to you she can no more be given.

HEROD

She's dead. Hell take her murderers! She was fair.
Oh, what a hand she had. It was so white,   150
It did the whiteness of the snow impair –
I never more shall see so sweet a sight.

NUNTIO

'Tis true, her hand was rare.

HEROD   Her hand? Her hands.
She had not singly one of beauty rare,
But such a pair as here, where Herod stands,   155
He dares the world to make to both compare.
Accursed Salome, had'st thou been still,
My Mariam had been breathing by my side.
Oh, never had I, had I had my will,
Sent forth command that Mariam should have died.   160
But, Salome, thou didst with envy vex
To see thyself out-matchèd in thy sex.
Upon your sex's forehead Mariam sat
To grace you all like an imperial crown,
But you, fond fool, have rudely pushed thereat   165
And proudly pulled your proper glory down.
One smile of hers – nay, not so much – a look
Was worth a hundred thousand such as you.
Judea, how canst thou the wretches brook

---

143   *smoothest brow* Compare Herod's accusations at IV.iv.17–20ff. In the madness of his grief, he begins the process of clearing Mariam's name.
145   *weeds* clothes.
157   *still* quiet.
159   *had I . . . will* 'if I had been in control of myself' or 'if I had been able to do what I wanted'.
161   *vex* become dissatisfied.
163–4   Compare Proverbs 12.4.
166   *proper* own.
169   *brook* tolerate.

That robbed from thee the fairest of the crew?   170
You dwellers in the now-deprivèd land
Wherein the matchless Mariam was bred,
Why grasp not each of you a sword in hand
To aim at me, your cruel sovereign's head?
Oh, when you think of Herod as your king   175
And owner of the pride of Palestine,
This act to your remembrance likewise bring:
'Tis I have overthrown your royal line.
Within her purer veins the blood did run
That from her grandam, Sarah, she derived,   180
Whose beldame age the love of kings hath won.
Oh, that her issue had as long been lived.
But can her eye be made by death obscure?
I cannot think but it must sparkle still.
Foul sacrilege to rob those lights so pure   185
From out a temple made by heavenly skill.
I am the villain that have done the deed,   *taking*
The cruel deed, though by another's hand.   *on*
My word, though not my sword, made Mariam bleed;
Hircanus' grandchild died at my command.   *blame*   190
That Mariam, that I once did love so dear,
The partner of my now-detested bed!
Why shine you, sun, with an aspect so clear?
I tell you once again my Mariam's dead.
You could but shine if some Egyptian blowse,   195
Or Ethiopian dowdy lose her life.
This was – then wherefore bend you not your brows? –

170   *crew* company, group.
178   *royal line* Mariam's family, the Hasmoneans.
179   *her* Mariam's.
180–2 *grandam . . . lived* The beauty of Sarah, the wife of Abraham, attracted the
       admiration of kings in her old ('beldame') age: see Genesis 12.10–20, 20.1–18.
182   *her issue* her descendants, specifically Mariam.
183   *obscure* dark (but also hidden from sight).
186   *temple* i.e. her body.
190   *died* ed. (did Q).
193–238 The play ends with invocations to the sun and moon that call to mind Cary's
       dedicatory verses 'To Diana's Earthly Deputess'. The symmetry is notable.
195   *You . . . shine* You might shine like this.
195–6 *Egyptian blowse . . . Ethiopian dowdy* Indirect references to Cleopatra. A blowse is a
       beggar's strumpet; a dowdy is a shabbily dressed woman.
197   *This was* This (dead woman) was.

97

The king of Jewry's fair and spotless wife.
Deny thy beams and, moon, refuse thy light,
Let all the stars be dark, let Jewry's eye   200
No more distinguish which is day and night,
Since her best birth did in her bosom die.
Those fond idolaters, the men of Greece,
Maintain these orbs are safely governèd,
That each, within themselves, have gods apiece,   205
By whom their steadfast course is justly led.
But were it so, as so it cannot be,
They all would put their mourning garments on –
Not one of them would yield a light to me –
To me, that is the cause that Mariam's gone.   210
For though they feign their Saturn melancholy,
Of sour behaviours and of angry mood,
They feign him, likewise, to be just and holy,
And justice needs must seek revenge for blood.
Their Jove, if Jove he were, would sure desire   215
To punish him that slew so fair a lass,
For Leda's beauty set his heart on fire,
Yet she not half so fair as Mariam was.
And Mars would deem his Venus had been slain;
Sol, to recover her, would never stick,   220
For, if he want the power her life to gain,
Then physic's god is but an emperic.

---

202   *her best birth* i.e. Jewry's most celebrated daughter, Mariam.
203   *fond* foolish.
204   *Maintain these orbs* Assert these planets (or, more specifically, celestial spheres).
211, 213   *feign* pretend. Some copies of Q read 'fame' and others, 'faine'. The play's preoccupation with appearances and deception makes the latter reading more plausible.
211–13   *Saturn . . . holy* Although Cary invokes the Greeks at l. 203, she predominantly uses the Roman names for the gods. Saturn was associated with the humour of melancholy and was also sometimes associated with the law.
214   *justice . . . blood* Compare with the more moderate sentiments of the Chorus at IV.viii.129–34. Herod's words have more in common with Exodus 21.12: 'He that smiteth a man, and he die, shall die the death.'
217   *Leda* The wife of the Spartan king, Tyndareus, Leda infatuated Jove and was raped by him in the disguise of a swan.
219   *Mars . . . Venus* Mars, the Roman god of war, was the adulterous lover of Venus, wife of Vulcan.
220   *Sol* Apollo, the sun god, was also god of alchemy and medicine (i.e. 'physic', l. 222). *stick* hesitate.
222   *emperic* charlatan, quack doctor.

The Queen of Love would storm for beauty's sake,
And Hermes, too, since he bestowed her wit,
The night's pale light for angry grief would shake,   225
To see chaste Mariam die in age unfit.
But, oh, I am deceived: she passed them all
In every gift, in every property.
Her excellencies wrought her timeless fall,
And they rejoiced, not grieved, to see her die.   230
The Paphian goddess did repent her waste
When she to one such beauty did allow,
Mercurius thought her wit his wit surpassed,
And Cynthia envied Mariam's brighter brow.
But these are fictions; they are void of sense;   235
The Greeks but dream and dreaming falsehoods tell. *mt.*
They neither can offend nor give defence,
And not by them it was my Mariam fell. → *she was too*
If she had been like an Egyptian, black   *beautiful*
And not so fair, she had been longer lived.   240
Her overflow of beauty turnèd back
And drowned the spring from whence it was derived.
Her heavenly beauty 'twas that made me think
That it with chastity could never dwell,

---

223   *Queen of Love* The Roman deity, Venus, goddess of sexual love.
      storm rage, protest.
224   *Hermes* The messenger of the Greek gods (known to the Romans as Mercury). He
      was also the patron of oratory and wit.
      her Mariam's.
226   *in age unfit* in an unworthy era.
227   *passed* surpassed.
228   *property* quality.
229   *timeless* untimely (but also with a sense of 'immortal', in part because her tale will
      be repeated over and again).
231   *Paphian goddess* Venus: see IV.viii.22n. above.
      her waste what was taken from her (but also with a sense of the waste of Mariam's
      beauty).
233   *Mercurius* see l. 224n. above.
234   *Cynthia* One of the names of Diana, the moon goddess, patroness of chastity. See
      Cary's dedicatory verse, 'To Diana's Earthly Deputess', above.
235   *void of sense* empty of meaning.
237   i.e. They (the Greek gods) can neither be offended nor protect anyone (because
      they are fictitious).
239   *Egyptian* Another oblique reference to Cleopatra: see ll. 195–6 above.
241–2 Compare with Herod's objections to drowning Mariam at IV.vii.16–20: Mariam's
      own beauty, not an external force, was the cause of her demise.

But now I see that heaven in her did link   245
A spirit and a person to excel.
I'll muffle up myself in endless night
And never let mine eyes behold the light.
Retire thyself, vile monster, worse than he
That stained the virgin earth with brother's blood.   250
Still in some vault or den enclosèd be
Where, with thy tears, thou may'st beget a flood,
Which flood in time may drown thee. Happy day
When thou at once shalt die and find a grave.
A stone upon the vault someone shall lay,   255
Which monument shall an inscription have,
And these shall be the words it shall contain:
Here Herod lies, that hath his Mariam slain.

                                              [*Exeunt*]

[CHORUS]

CHORUS

Whoever hath beheld, with steadfast eye,
The strange events of this one only day –   260
How many were deceived, how many die,
That once today did grounds of safety lay –
   It will from them all certainty bereave
   Since twice six hours so many can deceive.

This morning Herod held for surely dead   265
And all the Jews on Mariam did attend,
And Constabarus rise from Salom's bed,
And neither dreamed of a divorce or end.
   Pheroras joyed that he might have his wife,
   And Baba's sons for safety of their life.   270

---

246   Compare with Herod's tirade at IV.iv.17–20, 31–4. Here, in contrast, Herod reconciles Mariam's virtuous appearance with her inner virtue.

249–50 Herod compares himself with Cain, the murderer of his brother, Abel: Genesis 4.8–12.

251–2   See Genesis 6–9 for the flood sent by God to cleanse the world of sin. These lines also resonate with the Greek myth of Niobe, who wept incessantly for the deaths of her children. The image neatly links Herod's mourning with that of Mariam at the start of the play: see I.i.75 and note above.

258   *his Mariam* Herod will assert his control over Mariam even after both their deaths.

260   *one only day* The Chorus remind us that the play has upheld the classical unity of time.

269   *joyed* was joyful.

Tonight our Herod doth alive remain,
The guiltless Mariam is deprived of breath,
Stout Constabarus both divorced and slain,
The valiant sons of Baba have their death,
    Pheroras sure his love to be bereft   275
    If Salome her suit unmade had left.

Herod, this morning, did expect with joy
To see his Mariam's much-belovèd face,
And yet, ere night, he did her life destroy
And surely thought she did her name disgrace.   280
    Yet now again, so short do humours last,
    He both repents her death and knows her chaste.

Had he, with wisdom, now her death delayed,
He at his pleasure might command her death,
But now he hath his power so much betrayed   285
As all his woes cannot restore her breath.
    Now doth he strangely, lunatically rave,
    Because his Mariam's life he cannot save.

This day's events were certainly ordained
To be the warning to posterity,   290
So many changes are therein contained,
So admirably strange variety.
    This day alone, our sagest Hebrews shall,
    In after times, the school of wisdom call.

FINIS

276   *suit* petition (to Herod for leniency towards Pheroras).

285   *betrayed* misused.

294   *school of wisdom* Kelly identifies a reference here to the apocryphal Book of Wisdom,
      or Wisdom of Solomon, 'a text relevant to the play's key themes of martyrdom and
      monarchy' (Erin E. Kelly, 'Mariam and early modern discourses of martyrdom',
      The Literary Career and Legacy of Elizabeth Cary, 1613–1680, ed. Heather Wolfe
      (2007), pp. 35–52, p. 46).